CONTENTS

KU-737-614

ACKNOWLEDGEMENTS

I would like to thank L'Oréal Professionnel for their help and support throughout my hairdressing career, particularly Neil Cornay, Commercial Director, who is now both a friend and a great ally in our on-going relationship with a great supplier; Gill Pope, Educational Development Director, whose belief in the educational value of my business knowledge is unwavering; and Sam at Essence PR for our on-going partnership spanning over a decade.

I could not have written this book without the guidance and advice of Dean Laming, from Salon Gold Insurance, Paul Mattei and Terry Marchant at The Leaman Partnership, our accountants, and Jeremy Wakeling, our surveyor whose relationship has been invaluable throughout our dealings with landlords. I would like to thank my business associate at Ultimate Salon Management.com – John Jameson, for being the geekiest, brainiest and loveliest teccy on the planet. There are many people I admire greatly in this industry, and none more than the Phillip Rogers, Chairman of HABB and a true philanthropist as well as being the business driving force behind the Sassoon empire for many years, and Simon Ostler, ex-MD of Tigi and now working on his own projects, whose drive, determination and business expertise are second to none in this industry.

My team are always my rocks – my PA Sam Good for her unbelievable brainpower, myriad of skills and unending patience; Gavin Hoare, our Salon Manager for being the best in the business and the face of the salon and above all, our General Manager Julie Norman, who alongside me, not only helped formulate all the elements of this book during our two decade working relationship, but puts them into practice daily and never fails to be a constancy in my life, both personally and professionally. Also thanks to our wonderful management team at the salon; Mario, Nando, Crissy, Matt, Gina, Lou and Candice who help me take all the credit for our wonderful business.

Above all, I want to thank Richard, the best husband and father on the planet – whose goals, dreams and vision I never stop sharing; my father Peter and my mother Lorna for teaching me everything I know before I realised I needed to know it, and all my family for their love and support, including my children Elysia and Oliver, who I hope will follow in our footsteps one day.

Hellen Ward

BOOK 2:
MANAGING FINANCES

HELLEN WARD

About City & Guilds

City & Guilds is the UK's leading provider of vocational qualifications, offering over 500 awards across a wide range of industries, and progressing from entry level to the highest levels of professional achievement. With over 8500 centres in 100 countries, City & Guilds is recognised by employers worldwide for providing qualifications that offer proof of the skills they need to get the job done.

Equal opportunities

City & Guilds fully supports the principle of equal opportunities and we are committed to satisfying this principle in all our activities and published material. A copy of our equal opportunities policy statement is available on the City & Guilds website.

First edition 2012

ISBN 978 0 85193 214 9

Publisher Louise Le Bas
Cover design by Gloo Communications
Typeset by Select Typesetters Ltd
Printed in the UK by CLOC

Publications

For information about or to order City & Guilds support materials, contact 0844 534 0000 or centresupport@cityandguilds.com. You can find more information about the materials we have available at www.cityandguilds.com/publications.

Every effort has been made to ensure that the information contained in this publication is true and correct at the time of going to press. However, City & Guilds' products and services are subject to continuous development and improvement and the right is reserved to change products and services from time to time. City & Guilds cannot accept liability for loss or damage arising from the use of information in this publication.

City & Guilds
1 Giltspur Street
London EC1A 9DD

T 0844 543 0033
www.cityandguilds.com
publishingfeedback@cityandguilds.com

Picture credits

Bonce Salons; Carita Paris; Dan Csontos©; Fudge Hair; iStockphoto.
com; Kérastase Paris; Kéraskin Esthetics; London School of Beauty
Therapy; Richard Ward Hair & Metrospa; Toni & Guy.

Picture credits

Every effort has been made to acknowledge all copyright holders as
below and publishers will, if notified, correct any errors in future editions.

Bonce Salons: pp67, 146; **Carita Paris:** pp31, 67, 68, 73, 82, 90, 97;
Creative Nail Design: p70; **Dan Csontos©:** p62; **Fudge Hair:** p151;
iStockphoto.com: © 4x6 p38; © AdrianHancu p30; © AdShooter
p174; © adventtr p122; © apcuk p21; © arcady_31 p81; © blackred
p170; © blackred p176; © bunhill p30; © ChristianAnthony p143;
© claudio.arnese p165; © dfm_media p162; © DNY59 p20;
© dwphotos p111; © edelmar p156; © Eulenblau p56; © FredFroese
p132; © froxx p60; © Graffizone p85; © hidesy p150; © hrhportia p120;
© ISerg p21; © IvonneW p94; © jondpatton p108; © JordiDelgado
p104; © k_stuart p94; © koya79 p116; © lightkeeper p135;
© macrofocus p164; © MKucova p124; © monkeybusinessimages
p68; © Mr-Eckhart p129; © Neustockimages p110; © nicolas_ p127;
© NuStock p103; © olm26250 p22; © pagadesign p128; © Palto
p56; © patrickheagney p161; © PeskyMonkey p173; © Pgiam
p177; © Photoevent p120; © phototropic p122; © porcorex p184;
© Professor25 p170; © raphspam p114; © seanami p71; © StevePell
p26; © swilmor p105; © Talaj p70; © VialedSun p102; © wakila p176;
© webphotographeer p183; © wwing p18; © Yuri_Arcurs p96;
© zennie p26; **John Frieda:** p7; **Kraskin Esthetics:** pp149, 156, 174;
Krastase Paris: pp138, 145; **Richard Ward Hair & Metrospa:** pp6,
19, 20, 23, 33, 33, 37, 50, 50, 60, 62, 57, 74, 75, 75, 76, 80, 85, 92, 92, 93,
94, 97, 102, 105, 120, 123, 127, 144, 158, 160, 179; **The London School
of Beauty Therapy:** p71; **TONI&GUY:** p158.

ABOUT THE AUTHOR

Hellen Ward is co-owner of the Richard Ward brand, together with her husband, celebrity hairdresser, Richard. Hellen started her hairdressing career after leaving school at the age of 16 and doing an apprenticeship with a national chain. After working a column for a couple of years, Hellen was promoted to Salon Manager, then Regional Manager and finally General Manager of Harrods Hair and Beauty at the tender age of 23, before finally meeting Richard and opening their own business in 1992. Combining Hellen's business acumen with Richard's artistic skills, they have gone on to create one of the most successful, independently-owned hair and beauty companies in the UK. Hellen lectures and educates hair and beauty salon owners, both nationally and internationally, as well as running other companies outside the hair and beauty field. She has two children and lives in London.

Hellen Ward

FOREWORD

People often forget that running a successful salon is as much about getting the commercial element right as it is the creative side. Developing a sound business acumen is therefore equally as important as honing an artistic skill-set. The Ultimate Salon Management series focuses on the three crucial areas a salon owner or manager needs to succeed in; being on top of the finances is perhaps the most critical.

Hellen Ward clearly demonstrates her knowledge and wisdom to would-be entrepreneurs and shares her unique systems to help deliver tangible results through this enlightening book, which is a must-read to give you a real understanding of the figures and get a grasp on your profitability.

John Frieda

INTRODUCTION

Never has there been a better time to be in the hair and beauty industry!

Industry statistics tell us that our sector is showing sustained growth and that there are more than 35,000 salons in the UK alone. These employ more than 245,000 hairdressers, barbers, hair technicians, beauty therapists and nail technicians, in an industry that is worth over £5.25 billion per annum. The average price of services in our salons has increased by 90% over the last 10 years and, with the heightened media awareness about our profession, many hairdressers are becoming celebrities in their own right – with multi-million pound product ranges, brand endorsements and franchise businesses continuing to evolve and develop. Hairdressing has shaken off its image of being badly paid, lowly or servile and has reinvented itself as a credible, creative profession with a multitude of spin-off careers: PR, media, marketing, sales and commercial management, brand management, technical training, franchising and personal development, to name but a few.

This is all very impressive, but working in the hair and beauty industry is not easy. As has been found by the owners of the many small businesses (classified as employing 50 or fewer staff) that make up 80% of the employers of the British workforce, the expertise needed to run your own company is ever-growing. Running a salon involves many different skills. We need to have an understanding of HR, PR, marketing, training and education, and retailing and merchandising, as well as having an aptitude for the finances and commercial negotiations if we want our businesses to thrive.

The industry is labour intensive, with the staff payroll being our greatest expense, but also our biggest asset and one that needs careful nurturing and cultivating. Failure to do this can result in heightened staff turnover; this is one of the biggest risks to the financial security of our businesses, and arguably the surest way to potentially lose turnover and profits. We are hugely dependent on our team staying with us and building successful client relationships through delivering personal, one-to-one service. Constant, ongoing training and staff development is therefore essential.

In order to ensure precious rebookings and word-of-mouth recommendations, technical standards need to be second to none, client service must be flawless and the customer experience unrivalled. The industry is uniquely client-facing, so customer satisfaction is key. Yet research tells us that client loyalty levels are dropping. UK salons have over 80 million visits per year but, with 98% of unhappy clients switching salons instead of complaining, we have our work cut out to ensure standards are up to scratch.

In an increasingly competitive marketplace, our branding and PR needs to be well-researched and marketed if we are to succeed. The profession is constantly evolving, so being on top of trends is ever more vital; we need to research client demand for new technologies and innovations in the market if we want to keep our customers loyal. Merchandising and retailing can bring in large revenue streams which can be a vital part of our businesses. That said, positioning your brand against the competition is increasingly complex, as the market is in continued growth, with salons becoming more and more innovative and sophisticated and standards everywhere constantly improving.

Most salon managers or owners have worked their way up from apprentice level, honing their talents creatively and usually deciding to open their own salons because they are the busiest and best stylist or therapist. However, this may mean that sometimes the business side of things can get a little overlooked. All that wonderful, carefully cultivated creativity can mean we are less interested in the financial, commercial side of things. So it is no surprise then that statistics suggest some 1200 salons a year go out of business – often poor management skills being one of the most likely reasons. Managing a salon is a complex business and many would-be salon owners find there is a real lack of resources and practical help on hand.

From my own experience, most of what we learn is gleaned by living through the situations ourselves; this is certainly how it has been for me. I have had no formal management training or university education. I started as an apprentice and worked my way up to being a stylist, then salon manager, then regional manager before finally opening my own business when I was in my mid-twenties. I had no official training, and there were no management books like this one that had been written by someone with a real understanding of what it is like to be a salon manager or owner. In fact, I often left meetings with my accountant feeling unsure of what he was telling me because I was too embarrassed to ask him questions or admit that I was baffled by his terminology! I am sure I am not alone in this and that many of you need to know some basic financial facts so you can understand your own finances – even if you are not directly handling them yourselves.

What my career has given me is a diverse experience of every type of salon imaginable. I have managed salons with 125 staff in some of the country's most glamorous department stores, as well as salons with just two staff in less salubrious locations. I have worked with salon managers up and down the country and experienced a wealth of hairdressers, therapists and clienteles. I have worked hard to learn what made them all tick and understand the issues they faced. There were often many similarities, although sometimes the problems they encountered could not have been more different. Everything I have learned has come through experience – and this is what I am sharing with you in the course of this series of books.

My *Ultimate Guide to Salon Management* is here to 'hold your hand' and guide you through the complexities of owning or running a salon or spa. I am not a lawyer, solicitor, accountant, wizard mathematician or business genius, and obviously there is never any substitute for proper legal advice, but I am a successful salon owner and entrepreneur. My 'tried-and-tested' formulas and techniques can help to give you the systems and tools you need to ensure your business runs as smoothly as possible. I can tell you a little about everything you will need to know to run a salon well, but some subjects are so comprehensive that it is not possible to cover them in enough detail in a book like this. What I can give you is a snapshot overview and general understanding of all the areas you need to think about in order to really manage your business to the best of your ability.

It can be a lonely affair being a boss, but sometimes just knowing that we all experience the same dilemmas, issues and problems may be enough to give you the confidence to get where you want to go – or just point you in the right direction.

In my series of three books, we will look at the following key areas:
- Getting Established
- Managing Finances
- Team Performance

In the first book, *Getting Established*, Part 1 covers the nuts and bolts of what you need to know to open a salon – the setting up and the red tape aspects. Even if you are already established, reading this guide will act as a reference and a checklist to make sure you have got it all covered. If you are a salon manager, you may not need to actually undertake the tasks involved with setting up, but you will undoubtedly need to understand them as they will continue to be part of your job role. In Part 2, we look at finding your own brand identity and conveying that to your customers in the branding, marketing and PR sections. These vital elements of establishing your business image will become the blueprint for your planning and brand evolvement.

In this second book, *Managing Finances*, Part 1 looks at increasing turnover and my tried-and-tested checklists to make sure your productivity is maximised. In Part 2 we cover the equally vital area of controlling costs, to make sure your salon is as profitable as possible. Both elements are covered with hints and tips from my own business experience to ensure you are focused on the right areas to grow and develop your business.

In the third book, *Team Performance*, the first part is dedicated to creating and managing a team, using my systems to ensure that your team really is your biggest asset. Part 2 will look at monitoring team financial performance, ensuring your team are delivering to the best of their ability and you are tracking and evaluating their performance. The series is then complete and will hopefully provide you with a reference guide to every area you need to think about to manage your salon successfully.

Each book is full of tips, facts and examples to demonstrate the strategies that I have implemented in my 25 years of salon management. The aim is to demystify each element to make it easy to understand and introduce in your salons, and so enable you to maximise the productivity and profitability of your business. You will also find my '10 steps' – a set of golden rules and quick reference points to sum up the secrets of creating a brand, a profitable salon and steps to success. All of the books are written in 'hair and beauty speak', avoiding the jargon and psycho-babble with my dos and don'ts, useful words, tips and facts to help make understanding salon management as easy as possible and give you the complete guide to making your salon the best it can be.

Good luck and here's to many more entrepreneurs in our sector!

(Statistics courtesy of HABIA and L'Oréal Professionnel)

MANAGING FINANCES

This handbook forms the second part of my series of three, and looks at running the finances of a hair or beauty salon, helping you to get to grips with the numbers, to improve your profitability and productivity and to gain a real understanding of how to manage the money.

PREFACE

There have been many changes in the hair and beauty industry since I joined it as a 13-year-old Saturday girl, working in the salon where my mother was a stylist. As with many professions, it has evolved into a slicker, more professional and better run industry. Gone are the days of the busy stylist having to multitask and answer the phone in-between doing a shampoo and set – and gone are the shampoos and sets! Now we recognise that customer service is key and most salons employ receptionists and trainees to offer back up. The trend toward professional colouring has meant that most hairdressers and therapists are more knowledgeable and have experienced a more comprehensive technical training.

Many of the quicker and faster services we can perform nowadays are due to technological advances in the equipment and products now available. These continue to help us to offer more innovative, technical styling and beauty services – raising our productivity, improving our time management and enabling us to turn over more money. Some services have naturally declined as fashions change (perm anyone?) but when one technology dies out another takes its place. The advent of chemical straightening services and permanent blow-dries have given the hairdressing salon economy a real boost, just as hair extensions did almost a decade ago when they burst onto the scene. Time-saving colour development accelerators enable us to reduce the time length of technical services, for example, and maximise on our time-poor, cash-rich clients. Advances in technology and ingredients enable us to offer organic products and revolutionary technical developments which enrich the experience for our customers and enhance our performance delivery.

In beauty, the sector has experienced huge growth. Once the preserve of a few department stores, day spas and nail bars are now found on many high streets with grooming becoming a choice of spend for many women with disposable income. Beauty salons are no longer the 'off-shoot' of the hairdressing salon, with one grimy room at the back promoted as an add-on. Beauty has become a fully-fledged industry in its own right; and is no longer the poor relation to its hairdressing sister sector. There have been huge advances in the services available to offer. IPL (Intense Pulsed Light therapy) or laser hair removal have enabled us to compete with the Harley Street consultants and offer a much-needed service that delivers significant levels of income stream. Services like endermology and glycolic peels have opened up a whole new sector that a well-trained, professional salon can tap into. Huge beauty retail brands which have remained professional-only and 'not on the high street' both add to ancillary income and also help to encourage customer loyalty via repeat sales. With the culture of weekly manicures seeping into the British consciousness from our cousins across the Atlantic, nail salons are not just the preserve of wealthy women; the service crosses all social strata and the uptake in demand from men continues to grow.

Large revenue streams are being brought in from retailing professional products that out-perform their consumer counterparts and the added income and commission from advising home care for skin, hair and nails has become a vital element in the success of many salons. Of course, this is only possible because the clients themselves have become better educated about the benefits of salon performance products and are more in tune with spending their hard-earned money on the benefits of professional advice.

Professional-only salon services are vital to our industry performance – we need to constantly innovate to discover new ways to keep the client loyal to the salon so that they do not contemplate trying technical services at home. With technology developing rapidly, most savvy salon owners embrace the advances in our industry and are on the look-out for the newest and most advanced therapies, services , treatments and products to help them maximise their profitability and retain their competitive advantage.

PART 1
INTRODUCTION:
INCREASING
TURNOVER

It really is not rocket science! When it comes to the money, in order to maximise profitability there are two areas we need to focus on: increasing turnover and controlling costs. It is critical to have a good understanding of the financial aspect of business. We simply cannot leave it to our accountants to let us know the financial position once audited accounts are compiled. So is your turnover in April lower than the year before, for instance? If you only find out six months later, you cannot do much to impact on such figures. We must be tracking our finances (takings, spend, etc) daily, weekly and monthly to get a clear picture of how we are performing. Even if you have a book-keeper, it is vital that you yourself understand the money coming in and the money going out if you are ever going to make a significant impact on the figures. This is not just about what we spend; it is equally vital to track our income. So it is not enough to know you are 10% down on last year (or even 10% up!). We have to know how, where and – more importantly – why it has happened in order to manage our businesses effectively.

In this part we will look at ways you can raise the turnover of your salon – from setting a target and then analysing your turnover and your productivity, to promoting to existing clients and attracting new ones – using my tips and successful business-model formulae to ensure your salon is maximised financially. We will also look at how suppliers and manufacturer relationships can help you reach your target takings, and how you can benefit from being loyal to one brand.

Let's get cracking – show me the money!

CHAPTER 1
SETTING TARGETS

This chapter covers how to go about setting an achievable target for your salon – one that fits into your business plan and can be broken down into detail and revenue streams. This will help you to monitor your performance and easily establish where you are doing well and which areas need some work.

Turnover

The money that a business takes (not makes!).

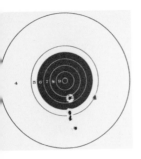

From your business plan, you will already have a good idea of your expected salon **turnover** per week, month and year. But the key to successful financial target-setting is to make sure they are broken down into enough detail, as each little element will come together to give you an overall idea of what your salon can achieve or where it is underperforming. It can be a little overwhelming to set yourself, for instance, a target of £400k per annum if you do not have an idea of how you are going to actually get there and which areas need attention in order to arrive at the figure. It is even more daunting not to reach your target *and* not to know why.

INITIAL BUSINESS PLAN TARGET

There are two main elements in setting your target. You need to look at:

- your maximum productivity/turnover assuming you are running at capacity (fully staffed, all productive space utilised)
- your minimum productivity/turnover that is needed to meet your fixed and variable costs and ensure you are breaking even, and the least turnover each team member must produce to do so.

It is important to calculate both maximum and minimum turnover and then to create a short- medium- and long-term forecast which will then become part of your ongoing business plan.

Your initial business plan target may be a 'back of a beermat' calculation, but it is a great starting point. The longer that you own or manage a salon, the more of a feel you will get for what is achievable; your 'gut instinct', once it develops, should be ignored at your peril.

WHAT YOU NEED TO TARGET

You should be setting the following targets.

Total salon turnover
- **whole-salon turnover per week** – broken down into days of the week to give you a clearer picture
- **whole-salon turnover per month** – broken down into your choice of financial reporting (how many weeks there are in your financial month or whether you work by calendar months)
- **whole-salon turnover per year** (a total of the months, however calculated).

Turnover by department

This is where the salon turnover above is coming from – colouring, cutting and styling, nails, beauty, retail, etc, broken down.

Turnover by individual

Finally, you need to look at who has to produce what in order to reach the salon breakeven figure. You can start by calculating the breakeven figure per individual to help you arrive at the whole salon target, and the gaps that emerge will help you to structure the rest of your business properly and set targets for ancillary (supplementary) turnover, for instance from **nonproductive** staff.

From experience, targeting the individual and days of the week turnover correctly will help to ensure the weekly, monthly and annual targets are being met automatically; so do not be daunted by the task. Tracking it by department will help you to work out your best-selling services and help your brand strengths to evolve. It may also help you look again at how you are utilising your **productive** space – for instance if your colour department is spilling out, it may be time to spend some money in rebranding and developing technical work as a speciality.

Nonproductive

Nonproductive staff do not produce turnover, but are still vital! For instance, apprentices, receptionists, laundry staff, office and management – anyone whose job is not directly dependant on bringing in money.

Productive

These are your turnover-producing team members and services. For instance, stylists, therapists, manicurists and technicians.

ISSUES TO CONSIDER

Things to consider, when working out your target, include the following:

- how much productive space there is
- how many chairs and sections you can operate
- how many beauty rooms or nail areas there are
- how many operators you can fit in
- how productive and occupied each operator is
- what the client/staff ratio is (ie how many clients each operator can do each day)
- what occupancy rate you are expecting staff to reach
- your projected average bill per operator
- your hourly rate of turnover per operator
- how often prices are going to go up and by what percentage
- salon opening days and hours.

Productive space

The square footage (or space in square metres) of your salon is a vital part of your calculation and working out the ratio of productive space to unproductive space is a worthwhile exercise. Your rent or premises cost/value (if freehold) should be governed by how much space is available to produce income, so it is useful to have a good idea of this. At the beginning, obviously, you probably will not be sufficiently established, or indeed have the capital to maximise all areas of space, until the business builds up and develops. Ideally, once the salon has started reaching its targets, utilising all productive space is vital. If you are taking over or running an already established salon, this is still a great exercise to undertake as it will give you an idea of what your maximum productivity could be. Remember, the long-term goal should always be that any empty areas should be utilised – otherwise you are paying 'dead' rent money on dead space.

Operational space

You should calculate how many chairs, sections and treatment rooms you can fit in. A lot will depend on your UXP (user experience) and brand ethos – so, for instance, if the client journey is top-of-the-range or premium, make sure you are leaving enough room between working spaces. Think of it rather like travelling premium, economy or first class on an airline; each has to work financially so if you are charging less you will need to fit in more seats, but you will not be able to charge more if the experience does not warrant it nor feels luxurious and spacious.

Number of operators

Once you have worked out how many stations, sections or rooms there are, you need to calculate how many staff will be needed to fill them. In the short term, they may not all be in use, so the number of operators you have is going to be a key figure and part of the calculation. If you are already at a maximum, you will have to think about how you can grow further. Can part-timers job share, for instance? Ideally, each section, room or station would be operational from the salon's opening hour until closing time, with every day optimised, too (that is **blue-sky thinking**!). But if – or when – you do reach capacity, it is worth considering how you can fill each area for the majority of the time.

Blue-sky thinking

Thinking without limits – it may be unrealistic, but it won't do you any harm to at least think in this way sometimes!

Operator productivity

Once you know how many staff you have producing income, then you can calculate how much per week they should be able to achieve. This will depend on their experience, where they sit in your price tiering system, the number of days they work and their work capacity. This exercise needs to be done on an individual basis. Think in terms of productive operators only and not total number of employees as some staff will not be solely income-producing (for example, office staff, juniors, receptionists) and any revenue they do generate will be supplementary (retail sales, for instance) and should not form part of the target-setting procedure.

Client ratio

Again, individually, you will need to calculate what the expected client/staff ratio is – the number of clients each operator could deal with per day maximum, and what the minimum number should be. Then, as with everything in your target setting, go somewhere in between to get your benchmark, depending on the individual and their track record once established.

Average bill

The average bill will also need to be worked out on an individual basis: how established (or busy) and how experienced each operator is will have a bearing on what they can charge, and therefore what they can produce in terms of turnover as an average per head. Average bill or average spend is normally the same as the value or cost of the most popular service performed by the operator – this is a good benchmark when doing your calculations.

Hourly rate

What we actually sell in our salons is time, so a good guideline in service terms is to work out the hourly rate per operator. For instance if you allow an hour for a cut and blow-dry and the stylist charges £50, it could be easily worked out that they could achieve £350 on a seven-hour average working day (with breaks of one hour). So if the operator works a five-day week they could bring in £1750 if they were performing at a maximum. But never set a target to this maximum – go slightly below and make it achievable. This means a sense of accomplishment can be felt about reaching the goal and there is not too much pressure on each individual – even if you choose not to make them aware of the seriousness of whether they hit their target or not.

Price increases

Increases in charges will affect whole-salon targets, average bills and individual performance. It should not be assumed that you will be able to instigate these regularly; much will depend on the salon performance, the competition and the economic climate, so do not build in an automatic 10% annual rise in your forecasting in case you cannot instigate it.

Trading days and opening hours

The amount of time the salon is open and producing turnover will affect its financial performance. You should, therefore, consider the salon opening hours and the total amount of time you are offering services when setting your target and thinking about maximum productivity.

REVIEWING TARGETS

I always find it easier to talk in weekly terms when it comes to targets. Some salons talk in monthly terms, to coincide with their payroll periods, but I find staff tend to understand and relate better to weekly turnover, and I know I do.

Targets should be reviewed and monitored constantly. Do not be afraid to re-jig your targets several times until you get them right. If they are never being achieved by anyone, something is clearly wrong and you need a rethink, quick! However, if you know your targets are realistic and some team members are reaching them easily and regularly but others are not, then usually it is an indication of an individual performance problem that needs addressing.

GROSS TARGETS

Contrary to my advice in Book 1 about always working in net and not gross figures, I always advise setting staff targets and daily targets in gross (inclusive of VAT). In other words, when talking to the team, use figures which refer to the gross amount taken through the till rather than net (after VAT has been deducted). It is much easier to visualise and communicate to staff members who need to track and monitor their performance for themselves and who may not understand the different figures.

EXAMPLE TARGETS FOR HELLEN'S SALON

In this example, we are going to look at my fictional Hellen's Hair and Beauty Salon, from Book 1.

In its business plan, it is expected to be able to reach £8000 gross per week in its first year, rising to £10,000 gross per week in its second year of trading. Hellen's business plan has calculated that there will be eight operators in total (six stylists, herself and a beauty therapist), who will average around £875 gross per week. Retail is targeted at £825 gross per week, which equates to just under 10% of the total salon turnover.

Breaking down the weekly total salon target by stylist
Note: You will see from this example that the stylists are in different pricing levels which affects their hourly rate and average bills.

The following calculations are worked out by:
• **Minimum productivity** – expected average bill x number of clients per week
• **Maximum productivity** – expected hourly rate x 7 hours (normal working day) x number of days usually worked per week
• **Total target** – is set somewhere between the two – minimum productivity plus between 10 and 50% depending on the individual and how established and experienced they are. These will need to be reviewed individually, and will be influenced by many factors like their work rate, length of service, pricing, motivation levels, etc.

Name	days wkd	average bill	hourly rate	no of clients p/w	min prod.	max prod.	total target
Hellen	4	£40	£50	24	960	1400	1000
Stylist 1	5	£35	£45	28	980	1575	1000
Stylist 2	5	£32	£45	28	896	1575	950
Stylist 3	4	£30	£40	25	750	1120	875
Stylist 4	5	£32	£38	25	800	1330	875
Stylist 5	4	£30	£38	20	600	1064	825
Stylist 6	5	£25	£33	20	500	1155	825
B/Therapist	5	£30	£35	25	750	1225	825
Sub total							**7175**
Retail/ancillary							825
Grand total							**8000**

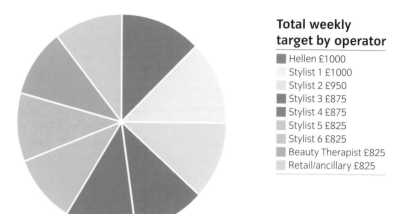

Total weekly target by operator

- Hellen £1000
- Stylist 1 £1000
- Stylist 2 £950
- Stylist 3 £875
- Stylist 4 £875
- Stylist 5 £825
- Stylist 6 £825
- Beauty Therapist £825
- Retail/ancillary £825

Breaking down the weekly total salon target by trading days

In the example below, Hellen's Hair and Beauty Salon turnover is broken down by day of the week according to staffing levels; for instance, most members of staff have either usually Monday or sometimes Wednesday off here. Doing this will enable Hellen to look at the overall turnover for each day and track whether she is on target, rather than waiting for individual results at the end of the week and totalling them up. Tracking this way enables her to implement last-minute measures and promotions if she is failing to reach her expected levels of turnover.

	Hair	Hair retail	Beauty	Beauty retail	TOTAL
Monday	640	60	0	0	700
Tuesday	945	90	150	15	1200
Wednesday	760	75	150	15	1000
Thursday	1000	100	180	20	1300
Friday	1455	145	180	20	1800
Saturday	1620	160	200	20	2000
Sunday closed					
Grand total					**8000**

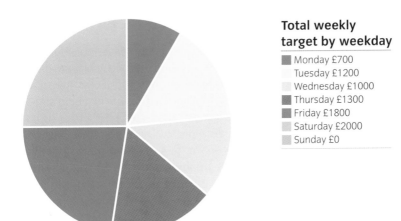

Total weekly target by weekday

- Monday £700
- Tuesday £1200
- Wednesday £1000
- Thursday £1300
- Friday £1800
- Saturday £2000
- Sunday £0

BREAKING DOWN INTO DAILY TARGETS BY INDIVIDUAL

In the example below, each individual has their weekly target broken down into daily levels, so they can also track and monitor their performance as they go. This is calculated purely by working out their total target, divided by the number of days they work. If they miss a day, through sickness, for example, this encourages them to work harder on the remaining working days to compensate, especially if they are financially motivated to do so.

Name	target	days worked	daily service	daily retail	TOTAL
Hellen	1000	4	250	25	1025
Stylist 1	1000	5	200	20	1020
Stylist 2	950	5	190	19	969
Stylist 3	875	4	218	21.80	896.80
Stylist 4	875	5	175	17.50	892.50
Stylist 5	825	4	206	20.60	845.60
Stylist 6	825	5	165	16.50	841.50
B/Therapist	825	5	165	16.50	841.50
Total staff retail				(156.90)	
Total desk retail					668.10
Grand total					**8000.00**

Note Retail is set at 10% of service target as an extra turnover level and, due to individual product prices, beauty retail should be targeted slightly higher than hair retail.

REVIEWING AND RESETTING TARGETS

Do not be tempted to review and increase (or decrease) individual and total salon targets too often. If they are being met and achieved, be realistic as to how and when you alter them; make sure that there is a tangible way in which they can be met and that it is not just blue-sky thinking on your part. The state of the economy will have a bearing on how and when you increase prices, which will have a direct impact on both your salon and your operators' targets. Remember also that this is not an exact science; it will vary greatly year to year and there will be many external influences over which you have no control. Individual targets should be reviewed, discussed and agreed during a scheduled appraisal with any team member – joint agreement is vital, especially if the employee is being appraised on their target achievement.

DOS AND DON'TS OF TARGET SETTING

Do:

- ensure targets are realistic and not the product of over-optimistic thinking
- remember you are rarely going to be performing at capacity levels so do not set targets too high
- reset any targets that are proving unreachable
- make sure targets are realistic and allow for a 'rainy day' such as staff sickness, school holidays, etc
- trust your gut instinct – nobody will know your team or your business like you do.

Don't:

- set targets net of VAT to staff, who will better understand gross when it comes to their performance; the same goes for daily whole-salon takings targets if you are informing receptionists or supervisors of the total-salon goal (always a good idea)
- change targets too often – let an established pattern of reaching targets comfortably before increasing
- forget to monitor your targets; they are only effective if you are tracking them all the time.

SUMMARY

Set your target somewhere between the least you need to
do to break even and the blue-sky thinking scenario of every
chair, room or section being filled every minute of the day.
Break this down into a short- medium- and long-term plan and
be realistic about reaching these milestones – give yourself
time to get there.

Not hitting a target is deflating for all concerned, so make
sure you are comfortably reaching the goal regularly
before you increase it – both for you as the salon manager
and for the individuals concerned. Review it professionally
and gain agreement that it is realistic and achievable
before implementing.

Breaking your target down per individual per week and
then per day makes it more real and easier for your team to
understand. Avoid talking to them in larger, monthly figures –
they will relate better to daily and weekly monitoring.

If targets are regularly not being met, then you need to address
and confront the problem. It will either be that targets are
over optimistic in the first place or there is an issue that needs
resolving. Find out sharpish!

CHAPTER 2
ANALYSING TURNOVER

This chapter covers how to break down your turnover and analyse your strong and weak areas so that you can establish which sectors of your business are performing and which need more focus in order to reach target figures.

MANAGING TURNOVER

Once you have set your targets, it is vital to track your performance against them. Statistics are only worthwhile and meaningful if they are kept up to date, are accurate and are checked regularly, otherwise they have no value. They also must be thorough and detailed enough, so make sure that checking your figures against your target becomes the most consistent aspect of your role as a salon manager or owner. Measuring your success or failure to reach the figures is a vital exercise and one that needs to become the most natural and 'automatic' part of your working week. It also needs to be actioned promptly – aim to finish last week's figures by Monday lunchtime. The longer you leave it, the smaller your chance of taking steps to address any concerns. It is essential to make the time to manage your turnover. Just spending 30 minutes per day means you can be completely on top of your salon's performance and have a real idea of where you are going. Often managers and owners are running a column too, but tracking performance against your targets should be delegated if you cannot do it yourself. Even if you do decide to delegate it, taking the time to understand the figures is vital and it is not something anyone can do for you.

ANALYSING DIFFERENT AREAS

Analysing turnover is different from analysing individual performance, which we will cover later. Think of your salon as if it were one of the leading supermarkets – you are assessing the performance of the bakery department compared with the pharmacy, the fresh fish counter compared to the frozen foods section, etc. By comparing all the different departments and revenue streams that your salon generates you are able to assess which are in growth, which are in decline and which need promoting and developing.

TRACKING PERFORMANCE

You need to know how beauty is performing, for instance, as a percentage of your total salon turnover, in order to assess whether you are in line with industry statistics, or whether you are falling behind; finding out enables you to take steps to impact on the figures. You are also tracking which areas are becoming more popular so you are ready to strengthen any strong areas of turnover, not just concentrate on any weak ones. For instance, some salons have become renowned for particular services because a switched on manager or owner spotted and focused on a growth trend then marketed it correctly and promptly, further cultivating an already strong area.

It's an interesting analogy that in the department store business, the allocation of floor space (square footage) and location are governed by turnover. For instance, perfumeries normally outperform other areas, both financially and in terms of customer volume, so are mainly located on ground floor entrances. The products that retail managers put near the places where everyone goes, like the doors, lifts, etc, should be determined by financial performance; this is often benchmarked against the total turnover of the store in percentage terms.

ISSUES TO CONSIDER

In our salons, we need to aim to cultivate the same ethos as in other retailers so that we are constantly monitoring all areas of the business and are maximising new opportunities. What you track and analyse will depend on the size of your business and the different services offered but, as a guide, here's what you should be thinking about.

Total salon turnover

Total salon turnover should be tracked in gross to check against targets or relay to team members, then turned into net figures in order to monitor properly.

Hair

Hair cutting and styling should be shown as a department, regardless of whether your stylists undertake their own technical work.

Technical

Technical work – colouring, chemical straightening, permanent blow-dries, forme, perm – all should be tracked separately from hair cutting and styling, even if some staff cross over into both. You should calculate their turnover on each and allocate to the relevant department to get really accurate figures.

Retail

Ancillary income

Money earned by a business through an activity that sits outside its normal core activity.

We need to know what **ancillary income** we are generating from retail as a total percentage of salon turnover, as this is relatively easy to impact on. It is worth breaking down your retail figure further into:
- beauty retail – retail turnover generated from beauty services
- hair retail – retail turnover generated from hair and technical services.

Beauty

If your salon provides beauty services only, this needs to be broken down further – into IPL (laser hair removal), waxing, facials, massage, body treatments, manicure and pedicure, nails (acrylic, etc). You can then discover your competitive edge and position your brand accordingly.

DAILY FIGURES

It is worth creating a daily figure book to give you a simple breakdown of your income and expenses, as well as the daily cash/account book (see Chapter 7). Filling this in every day can help you to track: total gross turnover, total banked and total bank differences.

Total gross turnover
This includes:
- hair (cutting and styling)
- technical
- beauty and nails
- retail, etc.

Total banked
This includes:
- cash total
- cheques total
- credit cards total.

Total bank differences
This includes:
- over/short amounts
- loyalty points/reward schemes redeemed
- petty cash total.

Daily Figure Book

Monday — date 20.2.12

Hair/Technical	£610.00	cash	£62.01
Beauty	£0.00	cheques	£0.00
Hair & Tech Retail	£60.00	credit cards	£587.50
Beauty Retail	£0.00		
Desk Retail	£20.00		
		Total Clients	17
TOTAL	£690.00		
Expenses	£37.99		
Points Redeemed	£0.00	% of Turnover	0.00%
Bank	£649.51		
Over/short	-£2.50		

Friday — date 24.2.12

Hair/Technical	£1,380.00	cash	£598.51
Beauty	£190.00	cheques	£0.00
Hair & Tech Retail	£161.50	credit cards	£1,195.25
Beauty Retail	£26.75		
Desk Retail	£50.00		
		Total Clients	46
TOTAL	£1,808.25		
Expenses	£16.49		
Points Redeemed	£0.00	% of Turnover	0.00%
Bank	£1,793.76		
Over/short	£2.00		

Tuesday — date 21.2.12

Hair/Technical	£910.00	cash	£270.51
Beauty	£140.00	cheques	£0.00
Hair & Tech Retail	£68.00	credit cards	£867.00
Beauty Retail	£10.00		
Desk Retail	£22.00		
		Total Clients	30
TOTAL	£1,150.00		
Expenses	£14.49		
Points Redeemed	£0.00	% of Turnover	0.00%
Bank	£1,137.51		
Over/short	£2.00		

Saturday — date 25.2.12

Hair/Technical	£1,700.00	cash	£532.81
Beauty	£150.00	cheques	£0.00
Hair & Tech Retail	£155.00	credit cards	£1,491.50
Beauty Retail	£20.00		
Desk Retail	£15.00		
		Total Clients	53
TOTAL	£2,040.00		
Expenses	£12.19		
Points Redeemed	£0.00	% of Turnover	0.00%
Bank	£2,024.31		
Over/short	-£3.50		

Wednesday — date 22.2.12

Hair/Technical	£705.00	cash	£162.53
Beauty	£129.00	cheques	£0.00
Hair & Tech Retail	£70.00	credit cards	£835.50
Beauty Retail	£15.00		
Desk Retail	£95.00		
		Total Clients	24
TOTAL	£1,014.00		
Expenses	£17.47		
Points Redeemed	£0.00	% of Turnover	0.00%
Bank	£998.03		
Over/short	£1.50		

Sunday — date

Hair/Technical	C	cash	
Beauty	L	cheques	
Hair & Tech Retail	O	credit cards	
Beauty Retail	S		
Desk Retail	E		
	D	Total Clients	
TOTAL	£0.00		
Expenses			
Points Redeemed		% of Turnover	#DIV/0!%
Bank	£0.00		
Over/short			

Thursday — date 23.2.12

Hair/Technical	£1,012.00	cash	£383.40
Beauty	£159.00	cheques	£40.00
Hair & Tech Retail	£90.00	credit cards	£868.75
Beauty Retail	£20.00		
Desk Retail	£50.00		
		Total Clients	36
TOTAL	£1,331.00		
Expenses	£36.60		
Points Redeemed	£0.00	% of Turnover	0.00%
Bank	£1,292.15		
Over/short	-£2.25		

WEEK TOTAL — w/e:

Hair/Technical	£6,317.00	cash	£2,009.77
Beauty	£768.00	cheques	£40.00
Hair & Tech Retail	£604.50	credit cards	£5,845.50
Beauty Retail	£91.75		
Desk Retail	£252.00		
	£0.00	Total Clients	206
	£0.00		
TOTAL	£8,033.25		
Expenses	£135.23		
Points Redeemed	£0.00	% of Turnover	0.00%
Bank	£7,895.27		
Over/short	-£2.75		

THE WHOLE PICTURE

Once you are regularly compiling your daily figures and information, you can then calculate the following across all of the sectors you are tracking:

- weekly turnover
- monthly/period total
- quarterly or 6-monthly totals
- annual totals.

This will really give you an excellent and detailed overview into your business and where you are going. It will help you to see the 'whole picture'. As with any statistics, the more data you have, and the more accurate it is, the more they will mean; but it is what you do with the information afterwards that is crucial.

Terms – net and gross
To remind you of the terms introduced in Book 1 Chapter 3, the gross turnover is that which comes into the till, before VAT is deducted; whereas net turnover is the figure after VAT has been deducted. To convert from gross turnover to net turnover, divide gross turnover by 1.2. So if gross turnover = £1800, net turnover = £1800 ÷ 1.2 = £1500.

I recommend that, as a manager, you always work with the net figure, but give targets to your staff in gross.

ANALYSING TURNOVER

Of course, there is no end to how much further you can break down your turnover. Large groups of salons have sophisticated monitoring systems so they can see at a glance which treatments and services are achieving what levels of turnover. However, make sure that you choose to monitor and track something which is sustainable; pick a few areas and make sure you track them regularly, consistently and correctly to build up some meaningful statistics, rather than jumping around all over the place, changing your mind on what to track or being sporadic, which will inevitably only serve to confuse you!

PERFORMANCE GUIDE

You will know your own salon's turnover far better than me, but as a guide, here is what I have benchmarked from my business experience. All figures shown are as a percentage of total net salon turnover.

Example: Hellen's Hair and Beauty Salon

We will use my fictional Hellen's Hair and Beauty Salon as our example again. All figures under the line are net of VAT.

		% of salon turnover	% of department total
Total gross weekly takings	£8000.00		
Total net weekly salon takings	£6666.67		
Hair (cutting and styling)	£3200.00	48%	
Technical (colour, etc)	£2133.34	32%	
Beauty	£666.67	10%	
Retail	£666.66	10%	
Hair retail	£399.60		60%
Beauty retail	£266.40		40%

Beauty retail is targeted at a higher ratio than hair, even though there are more hairdressers than therapists in our example salon, because beauty should generate more revenue due to higher individual product pricing. Our example salon aims at getting technical to provide one-third of the total salon revenue and retail to achieve 10%; these targets fall into the national averages, current statistics suggest.

HOW TO TRACK YOUR TURNOVER

First, establish what accounting periods you're going to use. I use 52 fiscal weeks, broken down into 12 periods which loosely coincide with the calendar months. For instance, period 1 might be January or April, etc (whenever your financial year starts), but accounting this way sometimes means calendar February can finish in 'March' so get used to calling them by their period numbers.

Two four-week periods are followed by a five-week one – so periods one and two last 4 weeks, period three lasts five weeks, periods four and five last four weeks, period six lasts five weeks, etc. There are four five-week periods in any 52 – week, 12 – period year. I find this easier than trying to go by calendar months, which may fall in the middle of a week. This way, each week is a total trading week.

Whatever method you choose, make sure you stick to the same periods and weeks each year so you can get a real idea of comparison in the second year, and so on. I call these my fiscal sheets. I file them in a clear plastic sleeved folder and update them every week, and always keep last year's figures at the back to refer to. Even if you are producing this data using Excel spreadsheets or a software system, it is great to print and file them so you have the information to hand and take with you to meetings, etc.

You can only manage and act on what you monitor so making sure you are thorough and diligent in recording the information is vital. It will take time to break down your figures but, if it becomes a natural start to your working week, you will soon find that you are keen to know the statistics and compare. The more data you input, the more you build up and the more you have, the more essential it will become. You will be able to run your business properly if you spend time collating the figures.

*Keep on top
of when all the
school holidays
in your area
are coming up.*

I find it helps to keep file notes on the fiscal weeks too – for instance if half term falls in week six in one year, and week seven the following year, you will have an instant explanation for a drop in turnover. If you do not do this, you will be racking your brains as to why there is a disparity.

ISSUES TO CONSIDER

There are quite a few factors that will have an influence on your turnover so you might want to log them on your analysis (fiscal) sheets. These include the following:

- school holidays
- bank holidays
- staff holidays (if you allow only one member of each department off at one time, for example, and you make an exception and allow two, this will affect turnover, so it should be recorded)
- Christmas closures
- extraneous circumstances – fire, flood, restricted access, no utilities, etc
- special holidays – royal wedding, jubilee or other celebration
- price increases
- staff training
- changes in VAT rates
- refits and refurbishments
- introductions of new services, treatments or brands.

There follows over the next few pages some sample Fiscal Sheets for our fictional salon, Hellen's Hair & Beauty Salon. You will see the grand total gives an overview over the two 6 month periods, and compares to the plan and last year's figures to give an instant record of the salon's overall performance. Then, on the following pages, you will see the turnover further broken down, so any areas that aren't reaching target or that have taken a dip from the previous year's figures become instantly visible and obvious by not only the turnover, but the number of clients and the week, too.

Hellen's Hair and Beauty Salon
Grand total

Figures include all retail

Period	Week	Actual	Plan	Last year	% plan	% LY	TY clients	LY clients
1	1	£6,689.25	£6,666.67	£6,213.45	0%	8%	196	191
	2	£7,001.56	£6,666.67	£6,912.23	5%	1%	210	220
	3	£7,100.25	£6,666.67	£6,500.00	7%	9%	211	203
	4	£6,952.34	£6,666.66	£5,932.56	4%	17%	204	183
Total		£27,743.40	£26,666.67	£25,558.24	4%	9%	821	797
2	5	£6,259.31	£6,666.67	£7,163.52	-6%	-13%	192	220
	6	£6,691.25	£6,666.67	£6,532.45	0%	2%	196	203
	7	£6,913.78	£6,666.67	£6,843.25	4%	1%	203	205
	8	£5,946.25	£6,666.66	£7,003.50	-11%	-15%	180	210
Total		£25,810.59	£26,666.67	£27,542.72	-3%	-6%	771	838
3	9	£5,931.45	£6,666.67	£5,423.65	-11%	9%	180	159
	10	£6,203.52	£6,666.67	£4,326.25	-7%	43%	182	127
	11	£6,925.56	£6,666.67	£5,264.35	4%	32%	203	154
	12	£6,694.35	£6,666.67	£6,921.25	0%	-3%	200	203
	13	£7,000.36	£6,666.66	£6,947.29	5%	1%	205	204
Total		£32,755.24	£33,333.34	£28,882.79	-2%	13%	970	847
4	14	£7,325.25	£6,666.67	£6,625.37	10%	11%	215	204
	15	£7,142.56	£6,666.67	£6,132.98	7%	16%	210	189
	16	£6,925.39	£6,666.67	£7,834.60	4%	-12%	203	240
	17	£6,715.85	£6,666.66	£7,346.26	1%	-9%	200	220
Total		£28,109.05	£26,666.67	£27,939.21	5%	1%	828	853
5	18	£6,627.56	£6,666.67	£7,932.25	-1%	-16%	194	250
	19	£6,253.59	£6,666.67	£6,953.00	-6%	-10%	184	218
	20	£6,546.89	£6,666.67	£6,592.78	-2%	-1%	194	205
	21	£6,899.99	£6,666.66	£8,356.25	3%	-17%	203	261
Total		£26,328.03	£26,666.67	£29,834.28	-1%	-12%	775	934
6	22	£7,156.85	£6,666.67	£6,521.35	7%	10%	211	203
	23	£7,124.58	£6,666.67	£6,793.56	7%	5%	210	210
	24	£6,923.52	£6,666.67	£5,932.64	4%	17%	205	185
	25	£5,931.56	£6,666.67	£7,456.25	-11%	-20%	175	234
	26	£5,900.89	£6,666.66	£7,001.25	-11%	-16%	174	219
Total		£33,037.40	£33,333.34	£33,705.05	-1%	-2%	975	1051
Six-month total		£173,783.71	£173,333.36	£173,462.29	0%	0%	5140	5320

Hellen's Hair and Beauty Salon

Figures include all retail

Period	Week	Actual	Plan	Last year	% plan	% LY	TY clients	LY clients
7	27	£7,111.23	£6,666.67	£6,045.54	7%	18%	211	188
	28	£7,923.23	£6,666.67	£5,132.59	19%	54%	235	160
	29	£7,532.26	£6,666.67	£6,206.50	13%	21%	230	195
	30	£6,922.22	£6,666.66	£6,423.58	4%	8%	208	198
Total		£29,488.94	£26,666.67	£23,808.21	11%	24%	884	741
8	31	£6,643.25	£6,666.67	£4,236.41	0%	57%	198	132
	32	£6,458.59	£6,666.67	£4,968.23	-3%	30%	182	156
	33	£6,135.65	£6,666.67	£5,964.23	-8%	3%	183	180
	34	£6,823.55	£6,666.66	£6,651.85	2%	3%	202	205
Total		£26,061.04	£26,666.67	£21,820.72	-2%	19%	765	673
9	35	£6,688.55	£6,666.67	£6,651.25	0%	1%	192	210
	36	£6,952.59	£6,666.67	£6,103.76	4%	14%	207	192
	37	£7,152.35	£6,666.67	£5,912.25	7%	21%	211	185
	38	£6,678.00	£6,666.67	£4,321.99	0%	55%	196	134
	39	£6,855.65	£6,666.66	£5,317.35	3%	29%	201	166
Total		£34,327.14	£33,333.34	£28,306.60	3%	21%	1007	887
10	40	£7,121.23	£6,666.67	£6,213.57	7%	15%	212	196
	41	£7,000.23	£6,666.67	£5,943.26	5%	18%	207	186
	42	£6,925.35	£6,666.67	£7,561.12	4%	-8%	205	235
	43	£6,521.21	£6,666.66	£7,001.25	-2%	-7%	194	217
Total		£27,568.02	£26,666.67	£26,719.20	3%	3%	818	834
11	44	£6,800.56	£6,666.67	£5,956.56	2%	14%	202	187
	45	£6,523.51	£6,666.67	£6,452.22	-2%	1%	196	200
	46	£5,964.45	£6,666.67	£7,123.55	-11%	-16%	178	222
	47	£5,879.25	£6,666.66	£9,843.16	-12%	-40%	174	309
Total		£25,167.77	£26,666.67	£29,375.49	-6%	-14%	750	918
12	48	£7,123.25	£6,666.67	£6,623.52	7%	8%	210	204
	49	£6,946.55	£6,666.67	£6,428.25	4%	8%	203	200
	50	£7,352.52	£6,666.67	£5,436.25	10%	35%	216	169
	51	£7,188.00	£6,666.67	£6,946.13	8%	3%	214	205
	52	£6,835.99	£6,666.66	£5,931.64	3%	15%	205	184
Total		£35,446.31	£33,333.34	£31,365.79	6%	13%	1048	962
Year-end total		£351,842.93	£346,666.72	£334,858.30	1%	5%	10412	10335

Hellen's Hair and Beauty Salon
Hair

Figures include all retail

Period	Week	Actual	Plan	Last year	% plan	% LY	TY clients	LY clients
1	1	£3210.84	£3200.00	£2982.45	0%	8%	114	111
	2	£3360.74	£3200.00	£3317.87	5%	1%	121	128
	3	£3408.12	£3200.00	£3120.00	7%	9%	123	118
	4	£3337.12	£3200.00	£2847.62	4%	17%	123	106
Total		**£13,316.82**	**£12,800.00**	**£12,267.94**	**4%**	**9%**	**481**	**463**
2	5	£3004.46	£3200.00	£3438.48	-6%	-13%	112	128
	6	£3211.80	£3200.00	£3135.57	0%	2%	115	118
	7	£3318.61	£3200.00	£3284.76	4%	1%	88	119
	8	£2854.20	£3200.00	£3361.68	-11%	-15%	97	121
Total		**£12,389.07**	**£12,800.00**	**£13,220.49**	**-3%**	**-6%**	**412**	**486**
3	9	£2847.09	£3200.00	£2603.35	-11%	9%	105	94
	10	£2977.68	£3200.00	£2076.60	-7%	43%	107	75
	11	£3324.26	£3200.00	£2526.88	4%	32%	118	89
	12	£3213.28	£3200.00	£3322.20	0%	-3%	115	118
	13	£3360.17	£3200.00	£3334.69	5%	1%	120	119
Total		**£15,722.48**	**£16,000.00**	**£13,863.72**	**-2%**	**13%**	**565**	**495**
4	14	£3516.12	£3200.00	£3180.17	10%	11%	125	119
	15	£3428.42	£3200.00	£2943.83	7%	16%	121	111
	16	£3324.18	£3200.00	£3760.60	4%	-12%	118	140
	17	£3223.60	£3200.00	£3526.20	1%	-9%	116	128
Total		**£13,492.32**	**£12,800.00**	**£13,410.80**	**5%**	**1%**	**480**	**498**
5	18	£3181.22	£3200.00	£3807.48	-1%	-16%	113	145
	19	£3001.68	£3200.00	£3337.44	-6%	-10%	107	127
	20	£3142.50	£3200.00	£3164.53	-2%	-1%	113	120
	21	£3311.99	£3200.00	£4011.00	3%	-17%	118	151
Total		**£12,637.39**	**£12,800.00**	**£14,320.45**	**-1%**	**-12%**	**451**	**543**
6	22	£3435.28	£3200.00	£3130.24	7%	10%	122	118
	23	£3419.79	£3200.00	£3260.90	7%	5%	122	122
	24	£3323.28	£3200.00	£2847.66	4%	17%	120	107
	25	£2847.14	£3200.00	£3579.00	-11%	-20%	102	136
	26	£2832.42	£3200.00	£3360.60	-11%	-16%	102	128
Total		**£15,857.91**	**£16,000.00**	**£16,178.40**	**-1%**	**-2%**	**568**	**611**
Six-month total		**£83,415.99**	**£83,200.00**	**£83,261.80**	**0%**	**0%**	**2957**	**3096**

Hellen's Hair and Beauty Salon
Hair

Figures include all retail

Period	Week	Actual	Plan	Last year	% plan	% LY	TY clients	LY clients
7	27	£3413.39	£3200.00	£2901.85	7%	18%	123	110
	28	£3803.15	£3200.00	£2463.64	19%	54%	137	93
	29	£3615.48	£3200.00	£2979.12	13%	21%	134	114
	30	£3322.66	£3200.00	£3083.31	4%	8%	122	116
Total		£14,154.68	£12,800.00	£11,427.92	11%	24%	516	433
8	31	£3188.76	£3200.00	£2033.47	0%	57%	116	77
	32	£3100.12	£3200.00	£2384.75	-3%	30%	106	91
	33	£2945.11	£3200.00	£2862.83	-8%	3%	107	104
	34	£3275.30	£3200.00	£3192.88	2%	3%	118	120
Total		£12,509.29	£12,800.00	£10,473.93	-2%	19%	447	392
9	35	£3210.50	£3200.00	£3192.60	0%	1%	112	122
	36	£3337.24	£3200.00	£2929.80	4%	14%	121	112
	37	£3433.12	£3200.00	£2837.88	7%	21%	123	108
	38	£3205.44	£3200.00	£2074.55	0%	55%	115	78
	39	£3290.71	£3200.00	£2552.32	3%	29%	117	97
Total		£16,477.01	£16,000.00	£13,587.15	3%	21%	588	517
10	40	£3418.19	£3200.00	£2982.51	7%	15%	123	114
	41	£3360.11	£3200.00	£2852.76	5%	18%	121	108
	42	£3324.16	£3200.00	£3629.33	4%	-8%	120	137
	43	£3130.18	£3200.00	£3360.60	-2%	-7%	113	127
Total		£13,232.64	£12,800.00	£12,825.20	3%	3%	477	486
11	44	£3264.26	£3200.00	£2859.14	2%	14%	118	110
	45	£3131.28	£3200.00	£3097.06	-2%	1%	114	116
	46	£2862.93	£3200.00	£3419.30	-11%	-16%	104	129
	47	£2822.04	£3200.00	£4724.71	-12%	-40%	102	181
Total		£12,080.51	£12,800.00	£14,100.21	-6%	-14%	438	536
12	48	£3419.16	£3200.00	£3179.28	7%	8%	122	119
	49	£3334.34	£3200.00	£3085.56	4%	8%	118	116
	50	£3529.20	£3200.00	£2609.40	10%	35%	126	98
	51	£3450.24	£3200.00	£3334.14	8%	3%	125	120
	52	£3281.27	£3200.00	£2847.18	3%	15%	120	108
Total		£17,014.21	£16,000.00	£15,055.56	6%	13%	611	561
Year-end total		£168,884.33	£166,400.00	£160,731.77	1%	5%	6034	6021

Hellen's Hair and Beauty Salon
Technical

Figures include all retail

Period	Week	Actual	Plan	Last year	% plan	% LY	TY clients	LY clients
1	1	£2140.56	£2133.34	£1988.30	0%	8%	63	61
	2	£2240.49	£2133.34	£2211.91	5%	1%	68	70
	3	£2272.08	£2133.34	£2080.00	7%	9%	67	65
	4	£2224.74	£2133.34	£1898.41	4%	17%	61	59
Total		**£8,877.87**	**£8,533.36**	**£8,178.62**	**4%**	**9%**	**259**	**255**
2	5	£2002.97	£2133.34	£2292.32	-6%	-13%	61	70
	6	£2141.20	£2133.34	£2090.38	0%	2%	62	65
	7	£2212.40	£2133.34	£2189.84	4%	1%	95	66
	8	£1902.80	£2133.34	£2241.12	-11%	-15%	65	68
Total		**£8,259.37**	**£8,533.36**	**£8,813.66**	**-3%**	**-6%**	**283**	**269**
3	9	£1898.06	£2133.34	£1735.56	-11%	9%	57	50
	10	£1985.12	£2133.34	£1384.40	-7%	43%	57	40
	11	£2216.17	£2133.34	£1684.59	4%	32%	65	50
	12	£2142.19	£2133.34	£2214.80	0%	-3%	65	65
	13	£2240.11	£2133.34	£2223.13	5%	1%	65	65
Total		**£10,481.65**	**£10,666.70**	**£9,242.48**	**-2%**	**13%**	**309**	**270**
4	14	£2344.08	£2133.34	£2120.11	10%	11%	69	65
	15	£2285.61	£2133.34	£1962.55	7%	16%	68	60
	16	£2216.12	£2133.34	£2507.07	4%	-12%	65	76
	17	£2149.07	£2133.34	£2350.80	1%	-9%	64	70
Total		**£8,994.88**	**£8,533.36**	**£8,940.53**	**5%**	**1%**	**266**	**271**
5	18	£2120.81	£2133.34	£2538.32	-1%	-16%	62	80
	19	£2001.14	£2133.34	£2224.96	-6%	-10%	59	70
	20	£2095.00	£2133.34	£2109.68	-2%	-1%	62	65
	21	£2207.99	£2133.34	£2674.00	3%	-17%	65	84
Total		**£8,424.94**	**£8,533.36**	**£9,546.96**	**-1%**	**-12%**	**248**	**299**
6	22	£2290.19	£2133.34	£2086.83	7%	10%	68	65
	23	£2279.86	£2133.34	£2173.93	7%	5%	67	67
	24	£2215.52	£2133.34	£1898.44	4%	17%	65	60
	25	£1898.09	£2133.34	£2386.00	-11%	-20%	56	75
	26	£1888.28	£2133.34	£2240.40	-11%	-16%	55	70
Total		**£10,571.94**	**£10,666.70**	**£10,785.60**	**-1%**	**-2%**	**311**	**337**
Six-month total		**£55,610.65**	**£55,466.84**	**£55,507.85**	**0%**	**0%**	**1676**	**1701**

Hellen's Hair and Beauty Salon
Technical

Figures include all retail

Period	Week	Actual	Plan	Last year	% plan	% LY	TY clients	LY clients
7	27	£2275.59	£2133.34	£1934.57	7%	18%	67	60
	28	£2535.43	£2133.34	£1642.42	19%	54%	75	51
	29	£2410.32	£2133.34	£1986.08	13%	21%	73	62
	30	£2215.11	£2133.34	£2055.54	4%	8%	66	63
Total		**£9,436.45**	**£8,533.36**	**£7,618.61**	**11%**	**24%**	**281**	**236**
8	31	£2125.84	£2133.34	£1355.65	0%	57%	63	42
	32	£2066.74	£2133.34	£1589.83	-3%	30%	58	50
	33	£1963.40	£2133.34	£1908.55	-8%	3%	58	58
	34	£2183.53	£2133.34	£2128.59	2%	3%	64	65
Total		**£8,339.51**	**£8,533.36**	**£6,982.62**	**-2%**	**19%**	**243**	**215**
9	35	£2140.33	£2133.34	£2128.40	0%	1%	61	67
	36	£2224.82	£2133.34	£1953.20	4%	14%	66	61
	37	£2288.75	£2133.34	£1891.92	7%	21%	67	59
	38	£2136.96	£2133.34	£1383.03	0%	55%	62	43
	39	£2193.80	£2133.34	£1701.55	3%	29%	64	53
Total		**£10,984.66**	**£10,666.70**	**£9,058.10**	**3%**	**21%**	**320**	**283**
10	40	£2278.79	£2133.34	£1988.34	7%	15%	68	63
	41	£2240.07	£2133.34	£1901.84	5%	18%	66	60
	42	£2216.11	£2133.34	£2419.55	4%	-8%	65	75
	43	£2086.78	£2133.34	£2240.40	-2%	-7%	62	69
Total		**£8,821.75**	**£8,533.36**	**£8,550.13**	**3%**	**3%**	**261**	**267**
11	44	£2176.17	£2133.34	£1906.09	2%	14%	64	59
	45	£2087.52	£2133.34	£2064.71	-2%	1%	63	64
	46	£1908.62	£2133.34	£2279.53	-11%	-16%	57	71
	47	£1881.36	£2133.34	£3149.81	-12%	-40%	55	98
Total		**£8,053.67**	**£8,533.36**	**£9,400.14**	**-6%**	**-14%**	**239**	**292**
12	48	£2279.44	£2133.34	£2119.52	7%	8%	67	65
	49	£2222.89	£2133.34	£2057.04	4%	8%	65	64
	50	£2352.80	£2133.34	£1739.60	10%	35%	69	54
	51	£2300.16	£2133.34	£2222.76	8%	3%	68	65
	52	£2187.51	£2133.34	£1898.12	3%	15%	65	58
Total		**£11,342.80**	**£10,666.70**	**£10,037.04**	**6%**	**13%**	**334**	**306**
Year-end total		**£112,589.49**	**£110,933.68**	**£107,154.49**	**1%**	**5%**	**3354**	**3300**

Hellen's Hair and Beauty Salon
Beauty

Figures include all retail

Period	Week	Actual	Plan	Last year	% plan	% LY	TY clients	LY clients
1	1	£668.92	£666.67	£621.34	0%	8%	19	19
	2	£700.15	£666.67	£691.22	5%	1%	21	22
	3	£710.02	£666.67	£650.00	7%	9%	21	20
	4	£695.23	£666.66	£593.25	4%	17%	20	18
Total		**£2,774.32**	**£2,666.67**	**£2,555.81**	**4%**	**9%**	**81**	**79**
2	5	£625.93	£666.67	£716.35	-6%	-13%	19	22
	6	£669.12	£666.67	£653.24	0%	2%	19	20
	7	£691.37	£666.67	£684.32	4%	1%	20	20
	8	£594.62	£666.66	£700.35	-11%	-15%	18	21
Total		**£2,581.04**	**£2,666.67**	**£2,754.26**	**-3%**	**-6%**	**76**	**83**
3	9	£593.14	£666.67	£542.36	-11%	9%	18	15
	10	£620.35	£666.67	£432.62	-7%	43%	18	12
	11	£692.55	£666.67	£526.43	4%	32%	20	15
	12	£669.43	£666.67	£692.12	0%	-3%	20	20
	13	£700.03	£666.66	£694.72	5%	1%	20	20
Total		**£3,275.50**	**£3,333.34**	**£2,888.25**	**-2%**	**13%**	**96**	**82**
4	14	£732.52	£666.67	£662.53	10%	11%	21	20
	15	£714.25	£666.67	£613.29	7%	16%	21	18
	16	£692.53	£666.67	£783.46	4%	-12%	20	24
	17	£671.58	£666.66	£734.62	1%	-9%	20	22
Total		**£2,810.88**	**£2,666.67**	**£2,793.90**	**5%**	**1%**	**82**	**84**
5	18	£662.75	£666.67	£793.22	-1%	-16%	19	25
	19	£625.35	£666.67	£695.30	-6%	-10%	18	21
	20	£654.68	£666.67	£659.27	-2%	-1%	19	20
	21	£689.99	£666.66	£835.62	3%	-17%	20	26
Total		**£2,632.77**	**£2,666.67**	**£2,983.41**	**-1%**	**-12%**	**76**	**92**
6	22	£715.68	£666.67	£651.13	7%	10%	21	20
	23	£712.45	£666.67	£679.35	7%	5%	21	21
	24	£692.35	£666.67	£593.26	4%	17%	20	18
	25	£593.15	£666.67	£745.62	-11%	-20%	17	23
	26	£590.08	£666.66	£700.12	-11%	-16%	17	21
Total		**£3,303.71**	**£3,333.34**	**£3,369.48**	**-1%**	**-2%**	**96**	**103**
Six-month total		**£17,378.22**	**£17,333.36**	**£17,345.11**	**0%**	**0%**	**507**	**523**

Hellen's Hair and Beauty Salon
Beauty

Figures include all retail

Period	Week	Actual	Plan	Last year	% plan	% LY	TY clients	LY clients
7	27	£711.12	£666.67	£604.55	7%	18%	21	18
	28	£792.32	£666.67	£513.25	19%	54%	23	16
	29	£753.22	£666.67	£620.65	13%	21%	23	19
	30	£692.22	£666.66	£642.35	4%	8%	20	19
Total		£2,948.88	£2,666.67	£2,380.80	11%	24%	87	72
8	31	£664.32	£666.67	£423.64	0%	57%	19	13
	32	£645.85	£666.67	£496.82	-3%	30%	18	15
	33	£613.56	£666.67	£596.42	-8%	3%	18	18
	34	£682.35	£666.66	£665.18	2%	3%	20	20
Total		£2,606.08	£2,666.67	£2,182.06	-2%	19%	75	66
9	35	£668.85	£666.67	£665.12	0%	1%	19	21
	36	£695.25	£666.67	£610.37	4%	14%	20	19
	37	£715.23	£666.67	£591.22	7%	21%	21	18
	38	£667.80	£666.67	£432.19	0%	55%	19	13
	39	£685.56	£666.66	£531.73	3%	29%	20	16
Total		£3,432.69	£3,333.34	£2,830.63	3%	21%	99	87
10	40	£712.12	£666.67	£621.35	7%	15%	21	19
	41	£700.02	£666.67	£594.32	5%	18%	20	18
	42	£692.53	£666.67	£756.11	4%	-8%	20	23
	43	£652.12	£666.66	£700.12	-2%	-7%	19	21
Total		£2,756.79	£2,666.67	£2,671.90	3%	3%	80	81
11	44	£680.05	£666.67	£595.65	2%	14%	20	18
	45	£652.35	£666.67	£645.22	-2%	1%	19	20
	46	£596.44	£666.67	£712.35	-11%	-16%	17	22
	47	£587.92	£666.66	£984.31	-12%	-40%	17	30
Total		£2,516.76	£2,666.67	£2,937.53	-6%	-14%	73	90
12	48	£712.32	£666.67	£662.35	7%	8%	21	20
	49	£694.65	£666.67	£642.82	4%	8%	20	20
	50	£735.25	£666.67	£543.62	10%	35%	21	16
	51	£718.80	£666.67	£694.61	8%	3%	21	20
	52	£683.59	£666.66	£593.16	3%	15%	20	18
Total		£3,544.61	£3,333.34	£3,136.56	6%	13%	103	94
Year-end total		£35,184.03	£34,666.72	£33,484.59	1%	5%	1024	1013

Hellen's Hair and Beauty Salon
Desk retail

Figures include all retail

Period	Week	Actual	Plan	Last year	% plan	% LY	TY clients	LY clients
1	1	£668.93	£666.66	£621.36	0%	8%	19	19
	2	£700.18	£666.66	£691.23	5%	1%	21	22
	3	£710.03	£666.66	£650.00	7%	9%	21	20
	4	£695.25	£666.66	£593.28	4%	17%	20	18
Total		£2,774.39	£2,666.64	£2,555.87	4%	9%	81	79
2	5	£625.95	£666.66	£716.37	-6%	-13%	19	22
	6	£669.13	£666.66	£653.26	0%	2%	19	20
	7	£691.40	£666.66	£684.33	4%	1%	20	20
	8	£594.63	£666.66	£700.35	-11%	-15%	18	21
Total		£2,581.11	£2,666.64	£2,754.31	-3%	-6%	76	83
3	9	£593.16	£666.66	£542.38	-11%	9%	18	15
	10	£620.37	£666.66	£432.63	-7%	43%	18	12
	11	£692.58	£666.66	£526.45	4%	32%	20	15
	12	£669.45	£666.66	£692.13	0%	-3%	20	20
	13	£700.05	£666.66	£694.75	5%	1%	20	20
Total		£3,275.61	£3,333.30	£2,888.34	-2%	13%	96	82
4	14	£732.53	£666.66	£662.56	10%	11%	21	20
	15	£714.28	£666.66	£613.31	7%	16%	21	18
	16	£692.56	£666.66	£783.47	4%	-12%	20	24
	17	£671.60	£666.66	£734.64	1%	-9%	20	22
Total		£2,810.97	£2,666.64	£2,793.98	5%	1%	82	84
5	18	£662.78	£666.66	£793.23	-1%	-16%	19	25
	19	£625.42	£666.66	£695.30	-6%	-10%	18	21
	20	£654.71	£666.66	£659.30	-2%	-1%	19	20
	21	£690.02	£666.66	£835.63	4%	-17%	20	26
Total		£2,632.93	£2,666.64	£2,983.46	-1%	-12%	76	92
6	22	£715.70	£666.66	£653.15	7%	10%	21	20
	23	£712.48	£666.66	£679.38	7%	5%	21	21
	24	£692.37	£666.66	£593.28	4%	17%	20	18
	25	£593.18	£666.66	£745.63	-11%	-20%	17	23
	26	£590.01	£666.66	£700.13	-11%	-16%	17	21
Total		£3,303.74	£3,333.30	£3,371.57	-1%	-2%	96	103
Six-month total		£17,378.75	£17,333.16	£17,347.53	0%	0%	507	523

Hellen's Hair and Beauty Salon
Desk retail

Figures include all retail

Period	Week	Actual	Plan	Last year	% plan	% LY	TY clients	LY clients
7	27	£711.13	£666.66	£604.57	7%	18%	21	18
	28	£792.33	£666.66	£513.28	19%	54%	23	16
	29	£753.24	£666.66	£620.65	13%	21%	23	19
	30	£692.23	£666.66	£642.38	4%	8%	20	19
Total		£2,948.93	£2,666.64	£2,380.88	11%	24%	87	72
8	31	£664.33	£666.66	£423.65	0%	57%	19	13
	32	£645.88	£666.66	£496.83	-3%	30%	18	15
	33	£613.58	£666.66	£596.43	-8%	3%	18	18
	34	£682.37	£666.66	£665.20	2%	3%	20	20
Total		£2,606.16	£2,666.64	£2,182.11	-2%	19%	75	66
9	35	£668.87	£666.66	£665.13	0%	1%	19	21
	36	£695.28	£666.66	£610.39	4%	14%	20	19
	37	£715.25	£666.66	£591.23	7%	21%	21	18
	38	£667.80	£666.66	£432.22	0%	55%	19	13
	39	£685.58	£666.66	£531.75	3%	29%	20	16
Total		£3,432.78	£3,333.30	£2,830.72	3%	21%	99	87
10	40	£712.22	£666.66	£621.37	7%	15%	21	19
	41	£700.03	£666.66	£594.34	5%	18%	20	18
	42	£692.55	£666.66	£756.13	4%	-8%	20	23
	43	£652.13	£666.66	£700.13	-2%	-7%	19	21
Total		£2,756.93	£2,666.64	£2,671.97	3%	3%	80	81
11	44	£680.08	£666.66	£595.68	2%	14%	20	18
	45	£652.36	£666.66	£645.23	-2%	1%	19	20
	46	£596.46	£666.66	£712.37	-11%	-16%	17	22
	47	£587.93	£666.66	£984.33	-12%	-40%	17	30
Total		£2,516.83	£2,666.64	£2,937.61	-6%	-14%	73	90
12	48	£712.33	£666.66	£662.37	7%	8%	21	20
	49	£694.67	£666.66	£642.83	4%	8%	20	20
	50	£735.27	£666.66	£543.63	10%	35%	21	16
	51	£718.80	£666.66	£694.62	8%	3%	21	20
	52	£683.62	£666.66	£593.18	3%	15%	20	18
Total		£3,544.69	£3,333.30	£3,136.63	6%	13%	103	94
Year-end total		£35,185.07	£34,666.32	£33,487.45	1%	5%	1024	1013

USING FISCAL SHEETS

Once you have established a system, you can start to use your fiscal sheets to plan various essential salon events and activities. For instance, you can plan promotions ahead of quiet times and be organised to arrange and steer staff holidays towards traditionally quiet months, where this is possible and practicable.

WHAT TO RECORD

I find that it is best to log slightly different information on each sheet. Once you have decided on your column headings, keep them the same from then on for easy reference. Do not track too much, or it will involve too much administration time and the chances are that you will not keep it up. Track the essential basics which give you a snapshot overview into what is going on.

Here is my guide about what to record – net – on a weekly, monthly, quarterly or six-monthly and annual basis:

Total salon turnover
You should include:
- this year's turnover; planned or targeted turnover; last year's turnover
- percentage up or down on plan; percentage up or down on last year
- number of clients this year; number of clients last year
- number of new clients in total.

This shows at a glance whether the business is up or down, and whether client numbers are sustained from the previous year. Then, do the same for each department.

Hair
You should include:
- this year's turnover; planned or targeted turnover; last year's turnover (not including retail)
- percentage up or down on plan; percentage up or down on last year
- number of clients this year; number of clients last year
- average bill this year; average bill last year.

Technical

You should include:

- this year's turnover; planned or targeted turnover; last year's turnover (not including retail)
- percentage up or down on plan; percentage up or down on last year
- number of clients this year; number of clients last year
- average bill this year; average bill last year.

Beauty

You should include:

- this year's turnover; planned or targeted turnover; last year's turnover (not including retail)
- percentage up or down on plan; percentage up or down on last year
- number of clients this year; number of clients last year
- average bill this year; average bill last year.

Retail

You should include:

- this year's turnover; planned or targeted turnover; last year's turnover
- percentage up or down on plan; percentage up or down on last year.

Then break down the retail sales further:

- hair retail
- technical retail
- beauty retail.

AVERAGE BILLS

Average bill calculation can be worked out in net or gross – use gross when talking to the team, and use net for your fiscal sheets, turnover analysis breakdown and all other accounting. Simply take your selected turnover and divide it by the total number of clients you have recorded. Using our example salon, for instance, if you are finding out the average bill for the whole salon, it will be the turnover divided by the total number of clients so:

> £8000 gross, £6666.67 net divided by 195 = £41.03 gross
> £34.19 net av. bill

WORKING OUT PERCENTAGES

To find out what percentage a figure is of another figure, use the following guide (using our example salon again).

If you wanted to find out what your retail turnover as a percentage of total turnover, just enter your retail turnover into your calculator, divide by your total turnover, and press the % key.

Use TY as an abbreviation for this year and LY as an abbreviation for last year.

So:
   if total net salon turnover is £6666.67,
   and net retail turnover is £687.50,
   retail turnover as a percentage of salon turnover is worked out like this:
      enter 687.50 divided by 6666.67 in your calculator, then press the % key – to get 10.3%.

   To find out what percentage increase or decrease this is on last year, use the following sum:
      $(TY-LY) \div LY \times 100$

   So when this year's retail turnover is £687.50,
   and last year's was £620,

   the sum to work out the percentage increase on last year is as follows:
      $(£687.50-£620) \div £620 \times 100 = 10.89\%$

WHAT TO LOOK FOR IN YOUR ANALYSIS SHEETS

Ideally, you are looking for plan achievement and growth on last year's figures. Even if you are up by whopping percentages (how nice!) in your salon total, you should be looking to discover where the growth has come from in order to maximise it. If you are down on last year or on plan overall, your analysis sheets can tell you whether it is a general trend across all departments (worrying), or there is a reason for it and it is down to the underperformance of one department only (less worrying – as you can find out the reason for this). If we look carefully enough, statistics can tell us what we need to know.

Trends and downturns take time to evolve, so ensure you are on top of tracking any figures that worry you to bring to light any potential downturns and, if a trend or pattern emerges, act swiftly. If a downturn or poor figure is bothering you and continues to decline for more than six weeks (the benchmark I use) it is a downward trend and needs prompt action plans put into place to redress the balance.

Particular issues

We will look at many of these issues later in the series, but here are some pointers to issues that may need consideration (we are focusing mainly on the negatives, of course – as the positives are not something to worry about, merely just a point of interest!).

- **Number of new clients is down on last year** – promotion and marketing should be the focus. Involve the team into thinking of new ways to encourage business.
- **Number of total clients is down on last year** – is this a trend or specific to one department only? Find out. If the trend is overall, create an immediate action plan.
- **Average bill is down on last year** – have prices gone up since? If so, this is worrying as it is a bigger decrease in real terms. Look at retraining staff to promote and upsell additional services. Revisit consultation training with your team.
- **Turnover is down on last year** – how many operators were there by comparison? Have prices risen? Are client volumes in decline too? Look at restaffing, promoting and introducing innovations to help encourage trade.
- **Turnover is down on plan** – are operator numbers as per plan figures? Are percentage decreases in line with other departments? Find out and establish the facts.
- **One department is underperforming** – bucking the salon trend. Compare this department with the total salon turnover as a benchmark – the issues should come to light fairly quickly. Is there a problem with the operators involved? Have a team meeting to involve the staff concerned into helping you discover some answers.
- **Turnover is OK but client numbers are down** – why? Are you short on operators compared with previous years? If prices have increased, this could be masking a problem. Investigate.

SUMMARY

It is vital to track and monitor your turnover and how it is made up. The composition of where revenue comes from will help form your brand values and USPs and will influence your marketing and advertising. However, the statistics only become meaningful if you are tracking the same figures regularly, accurately and consistently, so the data has to be reliable. It does not take long to work out the percentage of your overall turnover produced by each department, so ensure you spend time monitoring your revenue properly. Then act on what you find out; be on top of any poor performance –if you don't it will get on top of you!

CHAPTER 3
ANALYSING PRODUCTIVITY

In this chapter we will look at how to work out how productive your salon is and how to calculate your work rate. We will learn how to assess improving your productivity and maximising your potential turnover, looking at your staffing levels and best-selling services, and listing what you should be tracking to really get to grips with your salon's performance.

STAFFING LEVELS

My old boss used to say to me, 'Staff the salons for a Wednesday'. In other words, there might be some staff hanging around the staff room on a quieter Monday but you should be turning away business on a Saturday, so your mid-week staffing levels should be just about right – and that is how you know your levels of staff are correct. I have to say, I agree with this 'rule of thumb'. Staffing levels (ie the number of productive, income-producing operators you employ) are bespoke and individual to every salon. As an owner or manager, after a while and according to your experience, you will know instinctively when the time feels right to recruit and increase them.

However, until that happens naturally, the idiom above makes a good benchmark. I am often asked for my interpretation of the exact science of staffing levels – but this really does not exist. All I can give you is the different productivity indicators you should track to help you reach the right decision on when you have enough business to recruit or promote another operator from within. Waiting for your team to build and reach the required benchmarks is a good indication that it is time to increase your levels – employing staff to fill rooms or stations just because they are there is never a good idea.

HOW MANY STAFF?

It is no use employing enough staff in order to never turn away business on even the busiest day, as on the less busy days of the week they may not be fully or even partially booked and their salary may be costing you dear. Not only will they not be producing enough income to cover their payroll costs, but their motivation levels will drop and have a negative knock-on effect on other team members (something to be avoided at all costs).

Leave the people who really bring in the money free to concentrate on their customer and deliver a service that is second to none.

Busy, productive staff are generally happier because they are earning more and building up their clients; and if the team are happy, they certainly make life easier for the salon owner or manager. If you overstaff your salon you run the risk of too few employees sharing out minimal turnover and earning less, which is never good for morale or longevity of service. It is better to be moderately staffed so you have fewer staff earning more. On extremely busy days this may result in a little less turnover in the short term, so you may create more of a demand, but this should not have too detrimental an effect on the business in the long run.

If you have too few staff (especially where salons try to cut back on non-productive staff) the team may not able to deliver a consistency of service necessary to deliver the required UXP (user experience). You need the nonproductive service givers for the vital backup for the productive staff, enabling them to concentrate on bringing in the turnover and not worrying about other areas, such as reception, the backwash, laundry, etc.

KEY PERFORMANCE INDICATORS (KPIs)

This term is used by many different industries and sectors to assess the key areas of performance they are going to track and monitor within their businesses.

Here are some industry KPIs, which are vital to monitor in your salons:
- percentage request rates
- occupancy rates
- best-selling services
- **link-selling**, **up-selling** and referral rates.

There is no shortage of elements which you can track and monitor but, to assess productivity, keep to the key, critical points listed above. You should also make sure you share the information regularly with your team, so they are aware of the criteria they are being assessed against. We will look at individual performance in more detail later, but for the salon manager to assess work rates, etc, the points mentioned above are the vital, main components.

You may decide, for instance, to track what percentage of your clients are paying by card (not difficult to calculate and vital for negotiations over EPOS charges – see Book 1). Even more interestingly, it is great to record the percentage of customers who are having particular services or buying retail, particularly by operator.

Link-selling

The recommendation of naturally cohesive treatments – for instance, a client having an eyelash tint may think about having her eyebrows dyed too.

Up-selling

Recommending and prescribing additional treatments at the time of the service – for instance, turning a blow-dry client into a treatment, cut and blow dry.

Stylist	Amanda 23rd July		
8.30			
8.45			
9.00	X	Jones	
9.15			
9.30		CBD	
9.45			
10.00	X	Smith	
10.15			
10.30			BD
10.45			
11.00			
11.15			
11.30			
11.45			
12.00	O	Wallace	
12.15			
12.30		CBD	
12.45			
1.00	N	Cotton	
1.15			
1.30		CBD	
1.45			
2.00	O	Earnest	
2.15			
2.30			BD
2.45			
3.00			
3.15			
3.30			
3.45			
4.00	X	Fredricks	
4.15			
4.30			BD
4.45			
5.00			
5.15			
5.30		X 3	
5.45		O 2	
6.00		N 1	
6.15		Total: 6	
6.30			
6.45		% Request: 50%	
7.00			

PERCENTAGE REQUEST AND REPEAT RATES

It is vital to check these in the salon as an overall figure, as well as for individuals. The salon should be monitored in terms of percentage repeat clients, whereas the operators should be tracked in terms of percentage request clients. The percentage request is quite simply the number of clients, expressed in percentage terms, who have requested that particular operator. The salon's percentage repeat is merely the number of clients who have revisited the salon, in percentage terms. You know that those clients who are not **request clients** or **repeat clients** must be **new clients** or **transient clients**.

> **Example**
> For instance, if 10 clients book in any one day and seven of them have been to the salon before, then for that time period the salon is running at 70% repeat rate. That means three of those clients are new.
>
> If an operator deals with eight clients, and five of them have requested that operator, then they are running at 62.5% request rate for that day, and three of their clients are new to the salon, or transient, and do not mind who they see.

Request rates tell you what you need to know when it comes to tracking individual performance. I would expect to see a good operator be able to build to a 50% request rate after six months' continuous employment, and 70% after a year. Failure to reach these targets would cause concern and I would need to assess performance further. If we cannot guarantee that a minimum of seven out of ten clients will come back to a particular operator, we should not be risking sending precious new business in their direction.

Traps to avoid
When assessing team members, do not confuse regular clients with request clients – you need to make sure you are analysing the number of clients who are *actually requesting* the *individual*, not the salon as a whole.

Request

A client who has requested a particular operator.

Repeat

A client who has repeatedly visited the salon, but does not necessarily mind who they see.

New client

A client who is visiting the salon for the first time.

Transient client

A salon client who does not mind who she sees (not necessarily new).

Also, do not confuse high percentage request figures with good performance – you need to take into account the number of clients in total, too. For instance, if a team member regularly achieves 90% request but is only ever doing half the number of clients of another team member, the figure could be misleading and could demonstrate that the reception team have little faith in booking them new clients.

In addition, you should be sure not to fall into the comfort zone of thinking that a high overall percentage request of your salon is great. A good salon will see an average of 80% request or repeat business, which demonstrates that there is a healthy flow of new clients coming into the business, while the regular clients are continuing to repeat book (as eight out of 10 clients coming back). If the percentage of regulars is too high, this may be camouflaging that there is a lack of new customers coming in. Steps would then need to be taken to redress this and encourage new business – so be careful not to confuse the data.

There will always be a natural level of client shrinkage per operator; for instance, people move away, naturally migrate to other salons or just move on, however well run your business is and however hard you try. This figure particularly applies to individuals, so the goal is to encourage clients to move around and try different operators within your salon rather than leave all together. Because of this natural decline, even the best operators need a healthy flow of new business to tap into in order to sustain performance levels.

OCCUPANCY RATES

Perhaps the most critical benchmark of the salon and individual's productivity, the occupancy rate is a vital statistic. Rather like a hotel, or any other business that is selling time rather than actual product, the percentage of time the service is occupied in our salons is crucial. Hotels track their occupancy rate by the number of rooms booked at any one time. As salons, we need to track our occupancy by the amount of available time that is actually booked per person – out of all their possible time which is available to book. This is not always easy to track as many software systems do not automatically monitor this; but the calculation can be compiled manually and, once logged, is a vital element in analysing performance.

How to calculate occupancy rates

Simply divide the amount of booked time by the amount of possible productive time, and press the percentage key on your calculator.

For example, if Gemma works from 9am to 6pm – with an average of two hours break (one hour lunch, 30 minutes morning break and 30 minutes afternoon break), there are possibly seven productive hours of work in her day. She has clients booked from 9am to 12 noon (three one-hour appointments) then a one-hour break. There is no client booked at 2pm, but another client is booked at 4pm, and another at 5pm. Therefore there are two hours of possible productive time left unbooked, and five hours of time have been utilised.

So enter 5 ÷ 7 hours, and press the % key on your calculator: Gemma had a 71.4% occupancy rate on that day.

Name	% Occupancy
Stephanie	78.63%
Fred	76.88%
Joe	75.90%
Chrissy	74.87%
Sonia	73.43%
Priya	73.27%
Tom	71.64%
David	70.65%
Samantha	68.28%
Louise	67.68%
Mary	67.66%
Amanda	67.43%
Stephen	65.85%
Carol	65.86%
Kathy	64.72%

Occupancy benchmarking

I find that 70% occupancy is a good benchmark for both salons and individuals. Much will depend on whether you schedule breaks for your operators or if they prefer to have their breaks when they are not busy and you offer a more 'flexitime' approach to your working day. An operator should be hitting a minimum of 50% occupancy rate within six months of continuous employment, rising to 70% after one year. If no breaks are scheduled, these figures will decrease slightly. Hotels tend to aim at 65%–70%.

Tracking occupancy rates by individual is vital – it gives you a succinct overview of how team members are utilising their time. For instance, during a review, if occupancy rates are lower than expected, coaching in how to encourage link-selling and up-selling is a vital way to fill empty time and encourage staff to take responsibility for filling their columns through word of mouth and excellent service and technical performance. Request rates should be looked at in conjunction with occupancy rates as, if both are low, performance is a concern. A quick calculation by the reception at the end of each working day for each team member can give you a daily rate and help you compile a weekly average, then a monthly average, to give you a critical performance indication of your whole salon, and your individual team members.

BEST-SELLING SERVICES

It is important to know what your best-selling services are and to look at ways you can maximise them, if they are a core part of your turnover. It may be that you can streamline your implementation if staying price-competitive is an issue, for instance.

For example, if permanent blow-drying forms a large part of your technical revenue, you may wish to price tier to offer a more competitive price level by getting junior team members educated and trained to deliver the less technical elements of the service.

LINK-SELLING, UP-SELLING AND REFERRALS

Link-selling

If link-selling is to be successful, you must make your team aware of the importance of looking for and maximising treatments which sit together. For instance, a customer choosing a manicure may easily be recommended a pedicure, as the two treatments naturally gel together. It is worth coming up with a list of treatments and services which your salon offers that naturally dovetail and educating your team to look for potential clues during their customer consultations. So if a client is going on holiday and has booked a permanent blow-dry, you could offer a semi-permanent manicure or pedicure service, as she is clearly interested in treatments that deliver a long-term, hassle-free performance while she is away. Link-selling should always be carried out by recommendation and referral; avoid **cold-selling**, which will seem unnatural and contrived to the customer.

Cold-selling

Trying to sell something without a lead.

Up-selling

This is recommending and prescribing additional treatments on the day, or at the time of visit. Turning a blow-dry client into a treatment, cut and blow-dry, for instance, is a great example of how we can train and educate our teams to turn a slow day into a productive one. Developing this skill set through roleplay and honing consultation skills is key, as most up-selling will be based upon good recommendation and advice from your operators.

Referrals

These are equally vital to the salon's success and should be encouraged between the different departments. Colourists should be referring technical-only clients to try hair and styling services, and vice- versa, and beauty should cross-reference hair, too. Incentivising team members to refer their colleagues, especially if they are on similar price tiers, is a great way of maximising each client's individual spend.

SUMMARY

Make sure your staffing levels are cohesive and monitored at all times, especially when it comes to tracking individual performance. It is a big ask to get someone to perform if the business does not warrant their services in the first place.

Keep a set of KPIs as your assessing bible. Make sure your team are familiar with the terms and know what you are looking for, as well as how they are calculated, then regularly train and educate them in how to reach the criteria. Make sure you share information on these key performance indicators regularly and ensure that all data is up to date and accurate.

CHAPTER 4
PROMOTING TO EXISTING CLIENTS

In this chapter we are going to cover the most important and potentially the easiest method of generating revenue and increasing turnover – promoting to the clients you already have. We'll look at loyalty schemes, programmes and promotional ideas to maximise this most vital revenue stream and we'll profile the ideal salon client, and how we can aim to reach and tap into them.

If only as much time and effort was spent by salon owners on working to grow and develop their existing client spend rather than trying to attract new ones! It is a fatal error, and one I see continually on my travels. Many salons feel huge pressure to be chasing new customers when their focus should be on educating their team to maximise the full potential of their regular/repeat customer spend. By far the most efficient way to increase our turnover is working at increasing our existing customer spend in-salon. Some salons feel that they should be permanently discounting their services with introductory offers to new clients, when it would be far more effective for them to concentrate on finding ways of rewarding the loyalty and custom of the people who are already coming!

FIND/WIN VERSUS KEEP/GROW

If we go back to our ideal marketing analogy from Book 1:

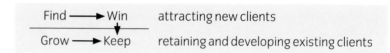

| Find ⟶ Win | attracting new clients |
| Grow ⟶ Keep | retaining and developing existing clients |

The keep /grow element is about looking to maximise what we already have by focusing on the existing clients who are proven spenders and already buying into our brand. This, by its very essence (as we have already won them over), is by far the easiest way to increase revenue. The find/win part is much more complex and much harder to generate revenue.

THE 80/20 RULE

Developed by the Italian economist Vilfredo Pareto, it is said that the 80/20 rule applies to most aspects of our life – for instance we wear 20% of the clothes in our wardrobes, 80% of the time. Or, that we spend 80% of our HR time dealing with 20% of our team. The 80/20 rule is found in many business textbooks, and it does seem to resonate and apply to most things. Likewise, with our customers, it could be said that 20% of our clientele produces 80% of our turnover. If this is the case, then the Pareto principle clearly demonstrates what potential we have by focusing on the remaining 80% of our existing clientele, aiming to increase their spend and encourage them to utilise all of the services the salon has to offer – rather than chasing around for a new and potentially unproven client.

THE IDEAL CLIENT

This exercise makes a great staff meeting for your team. It really helps them to understand the role that they, as operators, need to perform in order to maximise their takings, and in turn their earnings, and reach the key performance indicators you are benchmarking.

I often ask each team member to think about, or write down, who they perceive to be their ideal client – invariably they will choose someone who comes into the salon regularly and has a good relationship with them. Then I list down all the elements that would make my ideal fictional client.

In this example, I will profile a salon customer where there are beauty and hair services available. So an ideal client:
- ✓ has weekly blow-dries and manicures
- ✓ has hair-cutting services every six to eight weeks
- ✓ has colour services every six to eight weeks
- ✓ has permanent blow-dry services twice per year
- ✓ has waxing every six weeks
- ✓ has pedicures every four weeks
- ✓ has semi-permanent manicures and pedicures before holidays
- ✓ has possibly progressed to laser hair removal services
- ✓ has conditioning treatments and colour glosses every visit
- ✓ buys hair home care
- ✓ buys beauty home care
- ✓ buys dryers, brushes, accessories from the salon
- ✓ sends her partner in
- ✓ sends her children in
- ✓ purchases refreshments (if available)
- ✓ buys salon gift vouchers as presents
- ✓ signs up to the salon newsletter for exclusive offers, promotions and incentives.

And so on. You get the idea – there are probably lots of other treatments and services that you do that could be added to the list.

It is then extremely interesting to ask each team member to see how many boxes they can tick when thinking back to their ideal client – how many of the services on the list are they using? The results are often amazingly low (the 80/20 rule comes to mind). It really demonstrates that there are usually many areas left to exploit before we can ensure that everything that could be done to maximise the client spend is being done. Ongoing staff consultation training is therefore vital to making sure that as many boxes are ticked as possible. Often, we lose clients in our salons because we take their trade for granted and forget to treat each visit as if it was their first – assuming that we know what they want and do not need to continually review it in order to retain their business.

So we should be making sure that we get this right and working hard to retain our 'ideal client' by ticking all their personal boxes. This should be the focus long before we attempt to get in new business. Ensuring that all our branding, marketing and promoting are designed in order to attract this fictional customer is vital to our success.

CLIENT RETENTION

It has been shown that client retention improves with every additional service they use or buy. If a client is buying just one service from you, the chances of keeping them for longer than a year are only 50%. When you add a second service, that retention increases to 65%, and when a client is buying five services, you have over a 95% chance of keeping them for longer than a year. Other than receiving bad service, the likelihood is that the client will remain yours unless they move away or die.*

(Source: *Stop Getting By and Start Getting Rich* by Michael Cole)

There are many areas of salon revenue that a client will only tap into if they are advised and recommended. Therefore it is vital for financial success that we teach our teams to focus on working hard at honing their consulting and recommendation skills in order to capture this already captive audience. Retail is probably the easiest and quickest way to raise the turnover of a slow day and demonstrates that a thorough consultation has been implemented by our operators. I love Michael Cole's analogy that retail purchases in our sector are 'liquid tools' – the tools and implements we are giving to our customers to help them recreate the look at home.

It is also worthwhile pointing out that some of the 'unticked boxes' above are possibly being 'ticked' by another salon or shop. For instance, if a good beauty client never uses hair services, or if a regular client never purchases home care products, it is highly unlikely that they do not purchase/use them at all, merely that they are buying or using them elsewhere, perhaps because they haven't been diagnosed, advised and prescribed professionally or correctly by our teams.

Not only is the wider use of services a way to increase loyalty to the salon, it is a vital element in increasing loyalty to the individual operator. So referrals should be 'sold' to your team as a way of keeping their own clientele loyal, as well as helping to promote their colleagues. It also helps to breed a culture of ownership and responsibility of the team towards maximising their clienteles on an individual basis.

Example
For instance, Mrs Jones sees Ella for cutting and styling; Ella recommends Joanna for colour. Joanna recommends Gina for beauty, and Gina recommends Sue for manicures. Mrs Jones is now seeing four of the salon operators. Even if Ella left, Mrs Jones has now become loyal to three other team members, so the chances of her leaving the salon and following Ella are greatly reduced.

REBOOKING OR PREBOOKING?

Because the nature of our business is cyclical, our client visits run in cycles, too. Getting the client to rebook before they leave is the best way to ensure our future business and turnover is secure. It goes without saying (blue-sky thinking again here) that if every client rebooked before they left, we would be able to guarantee turnover and ensure our financial targets were met. Many salons, noting the drop in frequency of visits, have taken to encouraging the client to rebook before they leave. While in principle this is correct, I find the approach can sometimes be rather too forward and it may not be advisable to go for the blatant 'Shall I rebook you for next time?' before the client leaves. I do not expect to be touted for another visit before leaving my favourite restaurant, for instance. I need to decide for myself when I want to come back, unless I am being given a professional reason why I should or must revisit.

Statistics suggest that a client will tell three out of ten friends about a good salon experience, but seven out of ten about a bad one; this is worth sharing with your team, as it demonstrates how important it is that they work as hard as they can to provide excellent services and work hard to keep their clients happy.

TREATMENT PLANS

Treatment plans are an effective way of encouraging our clients to rebook. We need to train and educate our clients into prebooking appointments before they leave as much as we do our team, so creating a treatment plan (a programme of treatments prescribed by a professional operator) can mean that clients become more receptive to rebooking than if we use other more 'pushy' techniques and ploys.

Think of it rather like leaving the dentist – you never leave without being told, for example, that in six weeks' time you are due to see the hygienist for a scale and polish and that there is a filling which will need to be sorted out in three months' time. In our salons we need to establish the same mentality among our professionals. Each operator should leave the client with a clear idea of what they will need to have done and when in order to fulfil the long-term plan in place for their hair and beauty needs; this is their personal treatment plan.

As salon manager and owner, you should think about making this a non-negotiable part of the client consultation that you expect your operators to deliver, and ensure that the correct follow-up and advice that each operator undertakes becomes part of the UXP of your salons. An encouragement to book now in order to secure an appointment should be a subtle part of the client journey – not an obvious tout for business.

HOW TO CREATE A TREATMENT PLAN

Think about the following ideas in order to create a treatment plan for your clients:

- carry out a full and detailed consultation
- discover the client's long-term expectations and goals
- discuss a plan of treatments and a timeline to achieve the overall result
- schedule in the agreed appointments
- plan an ongoing grooming regime to deliver the results on a regular basis.

Rather than making other, more overt rebooking suggestions, I find that a professional, prescribed treatment plan as detailed above is an effective way of encouraging clients to utilise other recommended services and to keep their custom and loyalty. Education and training on techniques to encourage and develop this skill in our operators is essential to their own column-building. If the treatment plan is thorough and detailed enough, it acts as a business-building strategy for our teams. The canny operator is thinking about building their column, not just today or tomorrow, but realises that if they focus on filling their appointments in six weeks' time, everything else is taken care of already!

By encouraging, educating and tracking to make sure that a treatment plan is carried out by all your operators, a natural ethos of rebooking and professionalism will be developed. This will guarantee good results, both in increasing client loyalty and raising turnover from your existing customers.

CLIENT FILES

Whether you keep your client files manually or on a database, it is vital to use your client files to their maximum potential; they are not just a log of colour formulae or beauty treatments, although they are a great way of noting technical information, contraindications and other specific client information.

As with all data, the more detailed it is, the more you can use the information. Use your client files for creating your treatment plans, noting down products purchased so you can assess their effectiveness on the client's next visit, noting memorable occasions like birthdays, holidays or weddings and other personal information to encourage a great service ethos among your team.

Ensure you comply with the Data Protection Act at all times when handling client information: see http://www.ico.gov.uk for a helpful guide.

DETAILS TO NOTE

Make sure you log the following in your client files:
- name, address, phone number, mobile number, email address
- details of operators visited (may appear in client history)
- technical information
- products and services purchased
- courses of treatments purchased
- birthday
- treatment plans
- reward or referral schemes
- other personal information.

Specialised technical services may also need to include notes on: lifestyle, medication, diet and fitness, home care regime and **contraindications**.

Contraindication

A condition or circumstance to suggest or indicate that a particular technique, technical formula or service should not be used. For instance, client cannot have galvanic current in their facial if they have recently had Botox, nor can they use particular products if they are pregnant or diabetic.

HOW TO USE YOUR CLIENT RECORDS

You can use your client information in various ways, other than merely contacting them or texting them. Client history files should be able to tell you details of visits, spends, etc. You can use your database **proactively** (pre-empting opportunities) or **reactively** (responding to opportunities).

You can use client records to:
- monitor client visit frequency and lapsed clients
- look for trends in product purchases and services
- monitor buying habits
- gain marketing information
- identify promotional opportunities.

ADDED VALUE PROMOTIONS

As mentioned in the marketing section in Book 1, most successful, household name brands will never consider damaging their brand values by discounting. Think of premium beauty brands and how they often promote by GWP (gift with purchase); for instance, purchase two facial products and receive a free gift (normally something else from the range, like a make-up set or bag, all designed to increase brand loyalty and maximise future spend, of course).

Therefore, in our salons, we should follow their lead, as their sophisticated marketing is the result of much research into our spending habits. If I am a loyal customer of X brand, for example, I will not mind too much if I missed out on the promotion, as the product price was never reduced, so the value of the offer, although nice, was not critical to my spending decision. But I would be cross if it was discounted and I missed it! However, these companies would not consider devaluing and potentially damaging themselves by discounting their high-profile brands.

So, added-value promotions – incentives where a service is given an additional value for a period of time – are by far the best approach. For instance, a complimentary conditioning treatment with a cut and blow-dry service, running for a limited period of time, is far less damaging to our brand than discounting the cut and blow-dry. This is because discount periods have to end at some point, which will always result in bad feeling should the customer miss out. There is also the analogy that if a facial is worth, say £80 one week, why would it suddenly only be worth £50 the following week? Surely, the devaluation of the treatment can only be damaging. Not only that, but adding an extra service into the price as an incentive is a way of ticking another box and encouraging a client to use a service she might not be experiencing at present.

MARKETING ADDED VALUE PROMOTIONS

There are several ways we can make added-value promotions work: through the salon's Facebook page, Twitter feed, email marketing and in-salon marketing, ideally including well-designed posters and signage throughout the salon. To really be effective in our marketing to our existing clients, we should ensure that one key message is running throughout the salon at any one time. This will ensure that we can track and monitor what works, and also ensures that our branding is slick, professional and cohesive. Staff should be informed and even incentivised on offers through noticeboards, and staff meetings and suppliers can help us provide products in order to run the promotion in the first place.

Signage

Signage on section tops, rooms and work areas is most impactful and works best and provides a great talking point for the operator to introduce a potential new treatment. Make sure signage is neatly displayed in all general client areas, like the window, reception, waiting area, toilets, etc, so the message is clear and unequivocal. Once the promotion finishes, signage should be removed and replaced with a different offer from a totally different department.

It is always advisable to rotate offers by departments; for instance, a beauty offer like a complimentary eye treatment with any prebooked facial for the month of January, then a hair offer, then technical offer, then back to beauty for April for a different type of service offer, such as a GWP with body treatments. I arrange my promotional calendar at the start of the year to give suppliers and manufacturers a chance to be involved and to promote their chosen products and services as well.

In addition to the rapidly growing opportunities afforded by Facebook and Twitter, marketing these types of promotions via e-blasts is increasingly more effective than mail shots. Indeed, you can ask for your existing customers' email addresses as a way of offering them exclusive offers that are not available other than by newsletter, which also encourages the 'loyalty club' ethos we need to cultivate.

LOYALTY SCHEMES

Rewarding customers for their loyalty is essential, particularly in a challenging economic climate. It is easy to get waylaid and confused and chase the new business, offering rewards and incentives to get people through the door, but it is always far more effective to make sure existing customers are maximised and encouraged to stay loyal. Coming up with a reward scheme or loyalty points system is a great way to reward already loyal clients to stay with our salons, and not get tempted to switch brands or stray.

Most software systems can help you administer some sort of reward scheme where clients are given points for their spend, which can be redeemed against products and services that they can purchase at the salon. There are other ways you can use loyalty schemes, however. You can offer incentives where double points are issued, for instance, or offer extra points on any services booked in advance before leaving the salon; this is rather like an early booking discount for a holiday but, instead of giving money off, you are giving points to spend.

I find these incentives work really well and encourage people to maximise their spend and purchase things from you that they may have been buying from elsewhere. It also gives them a 'thank you' for their loyalty and custom, which is critical in the competitive marketplace.

REFERRAL SCHEMES

A 'recommend-a-friend' scheme is another good way to tap into that all-important word-of-mouth business. Referral schemes like this work through clients being incentivised to send in and refer their friends to the salon for treatments and services; thereby spreading the word and recommending people into the salon for you. I have never used referral schemes in my brand, but I can see that they work well for many salons as an encouragement and reward for gaining business by word of mouth. Systems can be administered by using vouchers that are redeemed by the original clients once the new client has visited.

SUMMARY

Make sure all members of your team understand the vital importance of working to capitalise on all the opportunities their already existing clients provide, both to increase their takings but also to encourage greater customer loyalty and so increase client retention. Train and educate them to take ownership of this element of their role to naturally grow their columns and takings.

Use your database to its full potential by noting not just technical data, but personal information too and recording treatment plans for future reference. Develop a loyalty programme to incentivise clients to maximise their spend in-salon.

Use added-value promotions to introduce new treatments and services to existing clients in-salon, and create a promotional calendar so manufacturers and suppliers can help you market and develop products and services in partnership. Value-added rewards are a great way to encourage client loyalty.

CHAPTER 5
ATTRACTING NEW CLIENTS

This chapter will look at tried and tested ways of attracting new business into our salons – what works and has proven efficacy, and which methods don't work so well. We will look at how we can bring in customers through associating with other local businesses and creating a local media profile, and what practices and procedures you need to establish bookings-wise to maximise the new client visit.

FINDING NEW BUSINESS

New clients can be one of our most precious resources, and attracting them forms the most vital part of our **find/win** strategy. Most companies spend huge sums in marketing and PR to bring in new business, yet some fail to implement systems to ensure their expenditure produces as much revenue as possible. The aim, of course, is to make the whole team aware that the new client visit is only successful if it results in a repeat booking.

There are several methods to use to get new clients through the door. In difficult trading times none are guaranteed success, but some do produce results. However, failure to educate our teams on how to cultivate this crucial business and turn new clients into regular customers will ultimately prove the exercise fruitless and our efforts (and expenditure) will be in vain. Many clients are shopping based on price alone, particularly in tough financial times; the 'deal chasers' are unlikely to become loyal, repeat business, however hard we try, so chasing them can be futile. This is why I would always advise concentrating efforts on growing existing business first and foremost.

UTILISING YOUR WINDOW SPACE

Always make sure that signage is professional looking, and that the treatments, prices and services you offer are clearly communicated. Opening times, web address and phone numbers should be easy to read and well displayed. Your USP or competitive edge should come across clearly from any signage – if it doesn't, it needs revisiting. Remember that your shop windows really are the eye into the salon when you are closed and to passers-by who are unfamiliar with your brand. Window signage can fade quickly so be sure to constantly update and change any advertising and marketing in your shop fronts.

Passing trade

Customers who walk or drive past the salon and decide to go in for a service, without having booked.

Keep it looking fresh – change specific (not generic or across brand) marketing and promotional material at least every six weeks. Marketing enticing promotions to attract new business through the facilities that you have readily to hand, like your shop window, is a relatively inexpensive and effective way of tapping into transient **passing trade** and enticing new business into the salon. One professional-looking poster that may generate some good, long-standing clients is worth as much as a huge spend in mail shots and random promotions.

INTRODUCTORY OFFERS

As you may have already gathered, I am not a fan of discounting services – I have seen too many cycles of continuous damage to brands instigated from that very first innocent offer. Once you get into the cycle of calendar discounting, it is tempting not to resist doing another 'colour sale' if you know you need to match last year's figures, or it if led to a huge spike in client numbers. It is not a good sign if operator columns are only busy during discounted periods, as staff will then tend to favour the periods of promotional activity and not take ownership for building their columns when prices are back to normal. Therefore, you can enter into a perpetual cycle of having to continue to cut prices, and you may find that good staff leave if they are suffering financially as a result of your pricing practice.

It also means that your team will need to work twice as hard to produce turnover from 50% off, services and their like – in that instance, having 8 discounted clients is the same as having 4 full price ones. If your team are financially incentivised, which they should be, they will not be in favour of discounting as it may result in doing your brand reputation and your chances of recruiting top operators long-term damage.

We do have a choice; even if many of our high street competitors tend to take the less sophisticated marketing stance of slashing prices and not thinking 'outside of the box' by merely discounting services. I would question how many of the customers that they attract can be turned into repeat business, however good they are. I also wonder whether the stress and the risk of devaluing and work rate is worth it, when the easier thing is to reward clients whose custom you are already appreciating. Like those adverts for car insurance and phone line rentals, where offers are not available to existing customers, I rather think they've got things the wrong way around. You should value your existing customers who keep coming back over new clients who only come in once for a discounted offer.

However, I am a fan of carefully selected introductory offers and incentives. They just have to be marketed and instigated in the right way and aimed at the right people in order to exercise damage limitation. There are ways to encourage new clients to try out our salons and services, but they must be carefully executed and continually measured for success; if they are not working, you need to change tack.

CONCURRENT OFFERS

Make sure there are not too many offers running at once – the worst-case scenario is to find an existing client paying full price, next to a new customer waving around four or five different offers and incentives. It can mean that your reception staff are so confused by 'Monday madness' or 'Wednesday stand-by' discounts that even they cannot work out which will result in the best end price for the client. It is not the way to make our valued clients feel that their loyalty is paying off! Running multiple incentives at the same time also means that an evaluation of what is working and what is not becomes far more difficult.

TARGETING LOCAL BUSINESSES

Rather than blanket discounting, I am all for creating incentives and promotions that are bespoke to carefully selected or like-minded companies. If you have large local businesses nearby, develop a relationship with the HR department to offer employees specially selected offers and incentives; their client base will provide a valuable foundation and word-of-mouth potential that you can tap into. These can be done privately and without the knowledge of your regular clientele and, better still, you can dictate when and how they are utilised.

SPECIAL INCENTIVES

Other than 'gift with purchase' offers or added-value promotions, some things to think about include:
- discounts with selected operators – for new team members or freshly-qualified staff to give their column a boost (graduates, for instance)
- discounts for selected services that you want to promote or which are underperforming – good for launching new treatments
- discounts on selected days – choose quiet days and times that need more take-up
- introductory offers like 15% off a first visit – or even better, a further or lesser discount off a second visit
- early-bird booking discounts for early 9am visits with selected operators or any other time that needs stimulus.

You will notice the common theme is that these offers and incentives are not blanket deals or available across the board. So you are still cultivating the ethos of creating a special 'club' feel to the promotion concerned and not risking damaging the selected areas as they are so specialised.

Other salons I know have offered stand-by bookings in the past where services become discounted if the client comes without notice. However, knowing that our aim is to get clients to rebook and encourage their individual treatment plan, this rather contradicts my ethos and so is not something I would recommend. We need to educate our clients into feeling motivated to rebook, not penalise them for it.

It is also worth tying up with local businesses to offer grooming seminars to staff upon their induction training, so they become regular clients of the salon and buy into your ethos as part of their company initiation. It is great if you offer discounts to employees of local retailers, too – 10% is a maximum – and you can negotiate this to become a reciprocal relationship so your team can benefit, too.

LOCAL ACTIVITIES

There are several local activities which your salon can be part of which can also bring an opportunity to get your brand into a captive market. Think about the following:

- bridal fairs
- charity fundraisers
- local events like fêtes
- recruitment evenings
- fashion shows.

Offering an incentive for people attending events like this is quite specialised and therefore carries no risk to damaging your existing customer profile. Print up some offer vouchers specific to the event and track the take-up. As with all promotions, being creative with your incentives is vital, so try and think 'out of the box'. Another quick and easy thing to implement is a stamped visit card, rather like the coffee houses offer, where a retail product or other incentive is received after a number of visits.

WHAT TO INCLUDE

It is worth using some magic words on your promotional material to protect you, such as:

- *Offer subject to availability* – meaning that you do not have to offer it if the team member/service/treatment/product is no longer available
- *Not available in conjunction with any other offer* – clients would have to choose which offer they wanted to have but cannot have both
- *Available with selected team members only* – when you do not want to offer a discount or promotion across the board.

ADVERTISING AND PR

As discussed in Book 1, national media is a hard nut to crack (and very expensive), but local media is normally a great way to encourage new business. Even local papers publish their own trend predictions now, so get a relationship going with your local paper's beauty editor or features editor to preview your team's ideas for hair and make-up trends or show them your photographic collections. Remember, they still work with lengthy lead times, so they will need information at least two or three months beforehand to secure coverage.

USE OF LOCAL MEDIA

Local property magazines are a great way to get glossy brand positioning too, and often you can secure a deal where you can receive editorial (unpaid space written by the journalist) in return for advertising (paid space) if you negotiate well. You can also use editorial copy to offer specially selected incentives for readers.

Inform local media of events like launches, fundraising activities or competitions within the salon to try and get editorial. You can get involved in community activities, like careers shows, which may aid recruitment too. Investigate local websites to offer introductory incentives or offers to e-traffic and drive transient business. There are many community websites that you can belong to where you can advertise and offer introductory discounts. Be careful not to pay for positioning your salon on sites like these – try to negotiate free-of-charge deals. Remember that they need you to belong and subscribe in order to make the sites financially viable with advertising, etc, from bigger, more established brands.

THE IMPORTANCE OF RECEPTION

Getting a new client to cross our thresholds is a task in itself, but our treatment of the client once she does is even more critical. The salon reception plays an integral role in acting rather like a matchmaking agency – finding out what the clients wants and needs then booking them to the operator best suited for matching their requirements and most likely to retain their custom. This is a skill that takes time to cultivate and such education is needed right across the team.

Employing and training a good receptionist will always pay dividends and is not an expense to be spared.

Receptionists need to have a blueprint or menu of the productive salon operators, so that they can quickly assess who should be given which client to maximise the chances of getting the match right first time. This critical exercise is often just left in the unskilled hands of a passing trainee who has been given the task of 'covering the desk' if the salon does not employ an adequate level of customer service assistants to book appointments. When you start to appreciate how retaining the possible new client is so crucial to the salon's success, and how hard we have to strive in our marketing and brand positioning to be able to welcome the new client into the salon in the first place, this seems nonsensical.

TEAM STRENGTHS

Keep a salon 'bible' of who does what – their strengths, weaknesses, technical expertise, etc, to help the reception team to get it right off the bat. For instance, not everyone in the salon will enjoy cutting children's hair, or specialise in hair up or scissor over comb. In beauty, some therapists shine at waxing or nails, whereas massage is a speciality of others. Logging all this and training it through to the rest of the team will not only help with recommendations but also ensure our treasured new bookings are delivered to the correct operator. Also, it is worth recording time-keeping and social skills. A client who is always in a hurry needs their pace and speed matched by their operator. A client who is at the salon for some laid-back pampering will not want to be rushed. Likewise, for the client who loves to natter, going to a stylist who does not do small talk but may deliver a technically excellent haircut won't encourage a revisit – matching people who are like-minded to their operators is a skill to be honed and developed.

A rather simple and obvious yet often missed trick is to ensure you highlight and differentiate between new and existing clients. Once you know who has not experienced your salon's services before, make sure they get the whole user experience – salon tour, proper introductions to their operators, familiarisation with their surroundings, explanation of your services, guidelines on what time they will finish, etc. Their visit close is equally important.

CLOSING THE VISIT

At the end of their treatment, do not forget to ask the client if they are happy. It is not necessary to fill out any feedback forms – a simple question from the most senior member of staff available or receptionist should be enough to suffice and get sufficient information to sort out any issues and aim to welcome them back into the salon soon. As with most things, it is not the system you use for tracking that matters, it is what you do with the information once you have it that is important.

If you get the vibe that there may be a problem, offer to resolve it. It may be a simple case of mis-matchmaking that can be easily resolved, or it may be more serious. We will look at other aspects of customer service later in the series to enable you to handle the feedback properly.

SUMMARY

We can best sum up this chapter with a list of do's and don'ts as follows.

Do:
• look at specific introductory offers and discounts which you can evaluate properly
• tailor your promotions to develop the areas of the business you want to concentrate on
• make it detailed in order to suit your salon, promoting the times and days you want to maximise
• cultivate relationships with local businesses, media and associations and run carefully chosen incentives with them
• teach your team how to make the most of new customers and train them to ensure rebooking is the goal, getting the treatment plan ethos into practice across all your team members.

Don't:
• be afraid to make offers specific to individuals or price tiers that you want to promote
• feel pressured to 'blanket promote' – you may be potentially damaging areas which are already performing well and good operators will not want to take a hit on their turnover and takings; avoid generic promotions – you may be discounting unnecessarily
• devalue your brand by giving away 'across the board' discounts which are promoted to the general public and which existing clients may discover.

CHAPTER 6
SUPPLIERS AND MANUFACTURERS

In this final chapter of Part 1 we will look at how to choose a supplier and why it invariably pays to be loyal to one predominant brand. We will also look at the different ways suppliers can help you grow and develop your business and the incentives, deals and discounts that could be available to help increase your turnover and cut your costs, depending on your spend levels.

RELATIONSHIPS WITH SUPPLIERS

Every business needs the support of suppliers, and they are perhaps as important to you as your customers. Your stock spend is their turnover, so it always makes sense to make sure that you spend as comprehensively as possible with one exclusive supplier. This should mean that you can negotiate good deals and gain benefits for your salon, rather than spending lots of small amounts with different companies and being a prized customer to none.

There are several large suppliers in the hair sector, with a much wider choice in beauty for professional products. Even if you are a small salon, by 'putting your eggs in one basket' and buying as many of your lines as possible from one company, your spend will not get diluted and you can benefit from better trading terms. Suppliers and manufacturers are always looking for custom, even in buoyant times, and their brands and offerings are constantly evolving, so finding a brand tailor-made for your salon's individual needs requires regular evaluation.

CHOOSING A SUPPLIER

Suppliers should be as appreciative of your custom as they are supportive of your brand. Your choice of product to use, stock and retail should be governed by the following elements:
- trust – that the company will deliver
- support – to help you generate the required turnover
- quality – should be assured
- good price points – so you can make enough margin
- good relationships – so that you feel well looked after and communication flows
- innovations and advancements in technologies – to compete well in our competitive market
- great marketing/PR and advertising for the products you retail, stock and use – to help you generate turnover
- long-term possibilities for the partnership of your salon and their products – so you have a clear idea of how the relationship could develop.

WHAT A SUPPLIER CAN OFFER YOU

A good supplier can offer support to your business and this can include the following:
- ✓ discounts – depending on your spend
- ✓ education – both creative and artistic, and business-wise
- ✓ ongoing product training
- ✓ marketing support for your in-house promotions
- ✓ PR opportunities – consumer and trade
- ✓ trade exposure for your brand
- ✓ incentives and competitions for your team
- ✓ external marketing opportunities – created and generated by them for their stockists
- ✓ credit terms (and flexibility if things are a little rocky but you have good trading history).

The level of support you will get will depend greatly on how much money you spend. Find out what you could get for buying more so you are aware of ensuring your spend is maximised and that you have benefitted in every way possible.

It goes without saying that you are looking for good quality and excellent brand positioning from your choice of products in order to generate maximum revenue and sales. You should also be conscious of the fact that your suppliers have a responsibility to help you sell the products you are buying from them, so you need to make sure they are proactive in following up the after-sales care to ensure products are selling well, both in retail and treatment terms.

WHAT SUPPLIERS WANT FROM YOU

In return, suppliers are looking to you for a number of things. They want you to:
- ✓ pay bills on time – or keep them informed of any problems with your account
- ✓ grow the business – for instance by agreeing to take on new products as they are introduced
- ✓ order regularly
- ✓ spend as much as possible with them and not dilute your potential spend with other companies
- ✓ recommend other potential customers
- ✓ be loyal to their brand
- ✓ be receptive to new innovations and products that they introduce
- ✓ get feedback from you about their products and services
- ✓ give them shelf space to promote and position their brands.

(It would be nice if we could charge suppliers for giving shelf space, rather like the supermarkets do; that is just wishful thinking at the moment, but who knows in the future!)

ORDERING

Stock-keeping units (SKUs)

Individual lines of a product range.

Your opening order is always going to be the most costly and needs careful calculation. Do not be bulldozed into ordering too many **stock-keeping units (SKUs)**. Negotiate a minimum opening order, if possible, and offer to review it regularly. Ask for uplift and exchange of lines that may be a mandatory part of the opening order after an agreed time period, so that you are not leaving your hard-earned cash to gather dust on the retail shelf.

As a service industry, we are mainly 'people-centred' in our sector, and our supplier relationships are often based on the people we deal with at the company concerned. Our decision making about which ranges to stock and use are not made solely on the products themselves; it is vital that you have a good relationship with your supplier and that there is an element of trust between you.

WHAT SUPPLIERS SHOULD NEVER DO

You do *not* want your suppliers to:
- ✗ take your relationship and spending for granted
- ✗ tell you about other people's turnover and spend
- ✗ tell other people about *your* turnover and spend
- ✗ tell you that you are underperforming compared to other salons
- ✗ be disrespectful of your time – if a meeting is booked, they must appreciate you are running a column and it has cost you money to see them – do not tolerate lateness or cancellations
- ✗ pressurise you into buying stock that they know you will not be able to sell
- ✗ fail to provide you with backup and support
- ✗ put their prices up too often (annually is enough)
- ✗ change their pricing without informing you (repackaging the number of items in a pack for instance, thereby sneakily putting the prices up)
- ✗ fail to provide you with consistency of service
- ✗ fail to provide you with a personal relationship
- ✗ fail to be on top of trends and industry developments
- ✗ stop asking their customers for feedback and acting on it
- ✗ stop listening to their customers.

If your chosen supplier is doing any of the above, point it out quickly and, if things do not change, switch to a supplier who will value your business.

PAYING FOR MERCHANDISING

Do not be persuaded to pay for merchandising and retailing that is company-branded by your supplier but is not dual-branded with your salon name on. Do you really want to pay them in order to promote their products in your salon? Shouldn't they be paying you for the free advertising? So many companies I know manage to get their customers to pay for their products stands, leaflet holders, etc. Refuse! They must provide you with these tools in order to get the range to sell – you should not have to pay for them. Offer to give them back any merchandising materials if the range fails or if you **de-list** their products – but do not pay out for them.

De-list

When you choose not to stock or buy a range any more.

MUTUAL SATISFACTION

Every salon has a different list of 'wants' from their supplier, and the good manufacturers and suppliers will meet with you regularly to find out where your business is going and what they can do or offer you to retain your custom. Some salons will purely be looking for education from their suppliers; others will be only interested in generating income from sales. Some may want promotional opportunities and others will want trade exposure. Whatever it is you are after, be clear to communicate it often and regularly to your chosen supplier. Make sure that the relationship works to your mutual satisfaction and best advantage so that everyone is happy and keen to carry on with it.

If a supplier does not bother wanting to find out where you are going, think about switching allegiances, as they are clearly not interested in helping you get there.

You should not think only in terms of retail ranges – your spend on salon-use professional products will probably be far more significant in the stock you need to buy to conduct hairdressing services; whereas in beauty it probably will invariably be a 50/50 split between what you spend on retail/professional stock. Buying professional or bulk products to use in the salon makes up a great deal of our stock spend, so make sure you are always thinking in these terms and not just about what you purchase to sell.

TYPES OF SUPPLIER

MANUFACTURER

You can buy products directly from your manufacturer. The large manufacturers will have sales reps that can visit you and take your order at your convenience.

WHOLESALERS

This is the company that sits between the salon and the manufacturer in the supply chain – they buy direct from the manufacturers and suppliers, and sell direct to the trade. Many are not open to members of the public. They normally offer a wide range of products and can deliver direct. Alternatively, you can shop at their outlets, rather like a 'cash and carry'.

We sometimes tend to forget another different sector of our purchasing – sundry goods – which can be substantial. Negotiate a good deal with your wholesaler to provide you with your salon essentials, like bedroll, disposable gloves, cotton wool, soap powder, etc.

DISTRIBUTORS

Some products, for example from overseas, have UK distributors who have a licence to sell and distribute the products in our marketplace, rather than the company having their own offices, supply chains, etc in the country. Be sure to negotiate well and ensure you are benefiting from the marketing, brand positioning, advertising and general terms of the parent company and that the distributor is going to offer you the same service levels.

MAXIMISING YOUR SUPPLIER RELATIONSHIP

PURCHASING POWER

Many small salons buy all their stock (sundry, professional and retail) from their wholesalers only, believing the myriad of offers will result in a cheaper price. This may sometimes be the case, but in general, it is far better to keep track of your spend and go direct to the manufacturer where possible to see if there is an incentive to buy direct from them. Remember, your wholesaler will not care which products you buy, as long as you are buying, whereas the manufacturer will want you to get the competitor advantage and potentially benefit from what you spend on their individual range.

CREATING A PARTNERSHIP

A good supplier/salon relationship is a partnership, which has short-medium- and long-term goals. Remember, you are only a good client if you tick all their boxes too – it is no use making demands if you are not a good customer, for example you do not order regularly or you fall behind in your invoice payments. Finding a supplier that suits your business is essential – you need the right mix when choosing the brands that you want to use and sell.

DOS AND DON'TS OF CHOOSING A SUPPLIER

Do:

- choose something that has a level of consumer appeal and customer awareness – you may not stock a well-known product exclusively in your area but, if it is a proven market leader, it is probably a safe bet
- go by personal recommendation – networking with other salons at events and finding out the thoughts and experiences of other salon owners and managers is a good idea
- have the right mix of products – some market leaders, some niche brands which you can stock exclusively, some mainstream ranges and some new innovations to give you a wide appeal
- ask your team – there is no point switching ranges if the team do not buy into the decision, you must get feedback from the people who are selling the products to your clients
- ask your customers – do not risk a decline in sales or turnover by failing to get feedback from the people who are buying or are the 'end user'
- get the right 'brand fit' that will sit well with your brand and your ethos – the retail products should be packaged to suit your salon and priced to appeal to your target client

SLA (service level agreement)

Documents that define each aspect of the level of service between a supplier/manufacturer and a customer; a working relationship contract to detail what both parties have agreed to and the terms of the agreement, ie payments, delivery details, etc.

- ensure the investment you are making in your opening order has a follow-up plan to ensure sales targets are achieved and that you are not overspending; stick to your budget
- insist on an **SLA (service level agreement)**, to get everything agreed in writing.

Don't:

- be afraid to negotiate terms – review your monthly and annual spend. Don't be shy about pointing out when you feel you deserve to be treated better and getting a revised deal
- take on new lines if you are unsure – see if you can get **sale or return** terms, or an agreement to uplift after a certain time period if sales are poor
- forget that overstocking your retail is as bad as not buying enough and your supplier will want to see you get your levels right – an empty retail area is unappealing to your customers and, conversely, overstocking is just as bad for your salon; there is no benefit to the supplier if stock is not selling, and you don't want your money tied up in dead stock
- assume your salon is too small and end up as a wholesale-only customer – find out if the suppliers will want to deal direct as you may be missing out on some good terms.

Sale or return

An arrangement under which, if the stock does not sell, the supplier buys it back from you or reimburses you.

HOW SUPPLIERS CAN HELP YOU

DISCOUNTING

If you reach your target spend with your supplier, you should be able to benefit from a structured discount programme to enable you to sell more at less cost. This needs negotiation on an individual basis. You may be able to negotiate some free-of-charge items too. Some discounts are calculated at source and some can be paid on a retrospective basis, where a percentage of your spend over an agreed time period is paid back to you. This can help with cash flow and be put towards other expenses.

BRAND POSITIONING

By stocking and associating your brand with ranges that have excellent consumer awareness, you should be able to generate retail turnover from transient or walk-in customers.

BESPOKE MARKETING

Suppliers can come up with GWPs (gift with purchase) incentives for your customers, help to cover the cost of marketing leaflets, posters, e-blasts, etc, for new services that involve their products and provide you with help and support for launching their new ranges or products to your customers. All these aspects will benefit you financially.

BRAND EXPOSURE

Large manufacturers are always on the lookout for up-and-coming brands which will be 'the next big thing' in the hair and beauty industry; every large salon chain or franchise started out with one single salon. Building a relationship at grassroots level from the start and growing and developing the business in partnership can give you a short cut to getting a trade profile. It can help you to 'think big' and achieve your long-term goals and aspirations.

EDUCATION

Training and educating your team invariably gives guaranteed results and can directly impact on turnover, perhaps by increasing an operator's prices, through promotion, or by aiding staff retention. Training will be allocated in ratio to the amount you spend, but courses will be available that are industry-specific. Product training should always be complimentary – do not get persuaded to pay for it.

EXPANSION

You may be able to get funding towards your future expansion from your supplier, depending on how good a customer you are to them and what your spend is. Contributions towards refits or openings are not uncommon among very high-spending salons.

SUMMARY

Your choice of supplier can be critical to the strategy you have for growing and developing your business. Take time to think about who you want to work with and choose a brand that has like-minded values and principles. It may be that you are looking for dynamism or you may want something traditional. You may be looking for guaranteed results or alternatively you may want to try something new and innovative.

Whatever you choose, do not be frightened to negotiate good terms and re-evaluate them on a regular basis. Remember that it is equally important to *be* a good customer in order to get maximum benefits.

PART 2 INTRODUCTION: CONTROLLING COSTS

We have now looked at all the ways you can increase your turnover, and, hopefully, I have given you some food for thought on how you can swell the salon coffers. Whether you own your salon, or are running a salon for somebody else, being profitable is vital to your own personal financial rewards and remuneration. Making the most of your income is essential to performance, but as the old adage goes:

Turnover is vanity, profit is sanity, and cash flow is reality!

Getting it clear in your head is key to being successful – it is irrelevant how much money comes through the till if just as much is going back out again. We need to think in terms of our bottom-line profit in order to stay financially secure and develop long term. Our cash flow is like the blood that flows round our bodies or the oxygen we breathe, it enables our businesses to function; whereas our turnover is the energy of our business, it is what we thrive on. Living without profit is like having an illness such as cancer; we can survive it in the short term. But living without cash flow – the money that we need to trade every day – is like having a heart attack. Very soon, our salons (like our bodies) will inevitably go into sudden shut down mode.

We must learn not to confuse turnover with profit. A salon can turn over £2m per year, but if it has £1,999,999.00 going out, it is not profitable. In contrast, a salon can turn over £400k per year, and if it makes £40k net profit, it is making 10%, and doing more than the salon with the larger turnover. So making sure our costs are in line is critical to our performance.

In the second part of *Managing Finances*, we will cover how to control our costs and stay profitable. We will look at how to understand the difference between cash flow, turnover and profit, and how to create your own management accounts so that you can track and monitor your performance as and when it happens, without having to wait for audited accounts from your book-keeper or accountant. Being in control of our costs is vital and understanding *how* we can impact them, even more so.

CHAPTER 7
SIMPLE ACCOUNTING

In this chapter we will look at how, as an owner or manager, you can compile a set of management accounts that will help you to control and direct your business. We will concentrate on how to handle simple book-keeping methods that will give you the data not only to monitor what is coming into your business, but also, most importantly, to analyse, most importantly, what is going out.

INCOME AND EXPENDITURE

Cash cow

Something that produces a steady flow of income.

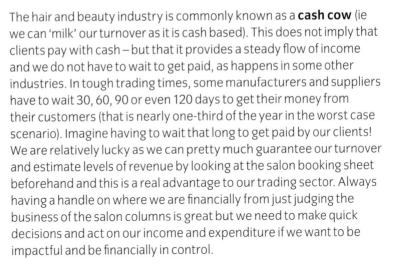

The hair and beauty industry is commonly known as a **cash cow** (ie we can 'milk' our turnover as it is cash based). This does not imply that clients pay with cash – but that it provides a steady flow of income and we do not have to wait to get paid, as happens in some other industries. In tough trading times, some manufacturers and suppliers have to wait 30, 60, 90 or even 120 days to get their money from their customers (that is nearly one-third of the year in the worst case scenario). Imagine having to wait that long to get paid by our clients! We are relatively lucky as we can pretty much guarantee our turnover and estimate levels of revenue by looking at the salon booking sheet beforehand and this is a real advantage to our trading sector. Always having a handle on where we are financially from just judging the business of the salon columns is great but we need to make quick decisions and act on our income and expenditure if we want to be impactful and be financially in control.

However, margins are tight, even for the high-end or premium salons and spas. The thin line between profitability and not making any money needs constant evaluation and monitoring. Even if you have an accountant or a book-keeper, or if your receptionist is the person who notes down the incomings and the outgoings, it is vital that you get a real understanding of the salon's spending and turnover by regularly looking at the figures yourself. It quite simply is not a job you can delegate if you want to make any inroads into changing things or turning your fortunes around. We cannot wait for the book-keeper to point out trends and patterns; we need to learn what to look for ourselves to track our spending and control our costs.

ACCOUNTING TERMS

There are different terms in accounting that you need to become familiar with.

Statutory accounts

These are a set of accounts upon which your tax liabilities are calculated, that are compiled by a registered accountant. If you are a limited company statutory accounts are filed annually at Companies House.

Book-keeper

A book-keeper is an administrator who can help you keep your accounts and records.

Registered accountant

A registered accountant provides professional services with regard to taxation and other liabilities and will usually be a member of a registered accounting body, for example the Institute of Chartered Accountants.

Registered auditor

A registered auditor is a member of a recognised accountancy body and is authorised to carry out and sign off an audit.

Audited accounts

If you are a limited company with turnover in excess of £6.5million the accounts will be subject to an independent review carried out by a registered auditor.

Management accounts

These are the accounts you use to manage and run the turnover and costs of your salon.

Double- and single entry-book-keeping

Book-keeping is merely the term used to record what is going in and what is going out.

- **Double entry** is defined as a system or procedure of recording both the 'debit' and 'credit' entry for each transaction in a traditional book-keeping system, ie where two entries are made enabling the book-keeping to balance.
- **Single entry** is defined as an analysis of each transaction to build up a summary, usually on a spreadsheet or manual cash-book.

DAILY CASH-BOOK

If you want a big cash-book, Collins Cathedral Analysis 150 4/16/2 – available from Amazon for example – has a good number of columns and pages.

I have always used a big, old fashioned cash-book to monitor and record daily what has come into the business, and what has gone out (or been spent). This is a continual statement of the current account of the salon (where the money is banked and the payments are made from). I also run a spreadsheet alongside, for extra security.

Your cash-book (or spreadsheet) acts as a summary and analysis of all your entries, including their VAT element, and is the basis and 'bible' for all your management accounting, giving you an 'at a glance' picture of the salon's performance. In your cash-book, you should record on a daily trading basis (log the date) and categorise the receipts (the 'ins') and payments (the 'outs').

RECEIPTS

The receipts, or **what goes in**, include:
- sales total
  - cash banked
  - cheques banked (some salons do not accept cheques any more)
  - credit card revenue received (you may want to break this down as it appears on your statement, if applicable) *This income should automatically appear in your account via BACS (Banking Automated Clearing Systems)*
- **total** of daily sales
- other income banked (invoices due, payments received, etc).

Note: all income will be gross or inclusive of VAT at this stage – you can take the total sales income and deduct the VAT to form the basis of your analysis sheet figures.

PAYMENTS

The payments, or **what goes out**, include:
- cash out (itemised in the correct column, once VAT is deducted and shown) – such as petty cash*
- **total** of cash expenditure
- bank out (itemised in the correct column, once VAT is deducted and shown)
  - cheques issued (cheque number referenced)
  - payments made (payroll, invoices, VAT paid, etc)
  - direct debits
  - standing orders
  - transfers between your current (cash) account to other accounts (for savings, etc)
- **total** of bank payments
- VAT to be reclaimed on total expenditure.

***Petty cash** is usually defined as being small, cash expenses like plasters, tea bags, and so on, that are purchased on an ad hoc basis. You can choose to have a petty cash tin, where regular sums are put in to purchase minor or incidental expenses, but it is just as easy to pay directly from the till and track the expense in your cash-book. However, regular payments should not be made here. You should avoid paying casual labour in cash – speak to your accountant, book-keeper or payroll clerk about anybody you wish to pay via the petty cash, as National Insurance and other taxes may be due on payments. All businesses have petty cash expenses, which are usually paid for straight from the till.

Keep petty cash to a minimum, monitor it closely, and keep VAT receipts for anything purchased.

LOGGING PAYMENTS OUT

The payments out column will be more complicated to log. You will need to list payments in gross (inclusive of their VAT element) then list the VAT you are reclaiming on the payment, or that has been invoiced, and put the net amount into the appropriate column – see the following examples.

Money in

Week ending:						
INS						
		subtotal	sales total	other income	total banked	
Monday	cash	£105.00				
	chqs	£25.00				
		£130.00				
	c/c	£520.50	£650.50		£650.50	
Tuesday	cash	£55.00				
	chqs	–				
		£55.00				
	c/c	£730.00	£785.00		£785.00	
Wednesday	cash	£15.00				
	chqs	£10.00				
		£25.00				
	c/c	£675.00	£700.00		£700.00	
Thursday	cash	£60.00				
	chqs	–				
		£60.00				
	c/c	£700.00	£760.00		£760.00	
Friday	cash	£45.00				
	chqs	–				
		£45.00				
	c/c	£500.00	£545.00		£545.00	
Saturday	cash	£55.00				
	chqs	–				
		£55.00				
	c/c	£1045.00	£1100.00		£1100.00	
Week Totals	cash	£335.00				
	chqs	£35.00				
	c/c	£4170.50				
	other income	–				
	Totals	£4540.50	£4540.50			

Balances	opening	closing				
Current:	£2330.00	£6870.00				
VAT Savings:	£2500.00	£2500.00				
IR savings:	£3050.00	£3050.00				
Rent Savings:	£1000.00	£1000.00				
Tax Savings:	£24000.00	£24000.00				
Profit account:	£4500.00	£4500.00				
Business card expenses:	£232.55	£630.95				

View online or download at www.cityandguilds.com/USM

Money out

OUTS

date	details	code	bank total	cash total	VAT	Transfers	dividends/ loan	payroll	purchases	rent	rates	service charge	ADV & PR	Insurance	laundry/ cleaning	heat/ light	Tel & Stat	refuse	sundry	repairs & renew	bank charges	accountants	legal	cars	bupa	shoots/ shows	pensions	c/c comm
Monday	Flowers			25.00															25.00									
Weds	Magazines			55.00															55.00									
Thurs	Stamps & Postage			20.00													20.00											
Friday	Coffee			3.50	0.45														3.05									
	Plasters			1.50	0.19														1.31									
	Peroxide			2.00	0.26				1.74																			
	Cleaning fluid			13.00	1.69										11.31													
	Picture Frames			25.00	3.26								21.74															
	Rent	DD	1150.00		150.00					1000.00																		
	L'Oréal	254	1250.00		163.04				1086.96																			
Saturday	Light Bulbs			14.50	1.89											12.61												
Totals			£2400.00	£159.50	£320.78	£-	£-	£-	£1088.70	£1000.00	£-	£-	£21.74	£-	£11.31	£12.61	£20.00	£-	£84.36	£-	£-	£-	£-	£-	£-	£-	£-	£-
	Grand total bank & Cash		£2559.50																									
	Grand total columns		£2599.50																									

View online or download at www.cityandguilds.com/USM

Expenditure categories

Across the top of your cash-book will be a series of categories in which to file and categorise each single item of your expenditure and the net payment amounts. Here are the ones I suggest you think about using:

- purchases (stock spend)
- telephone and stationery
- salaries and PAYE
- rent, rates, insurance and refuse (these will not be made that often, so you will be able to differentiate which is which by looking at the payee name)
- light and heat (power)
- laundry and cleaning
- advertising and PR (you can include marketing expenditure here)
- repairs and renewals (maintenance, etc)
- credit card commission (EPOS charges)
- self-employed contractors (if applicable)
- sundry costs (all other costs are listed here, for instance, entertaining, service charges, flowers, taxis, refunds, bank charges, etc) – log the details of the costs here too for future reference, as sundry costs will vary.

If you are using a software system or only using spreadsheets instead of an actual book, you can add more columns and break them down further. For example:

- dividends/loan repayments
- rent or franchise fees
- rates – business rates and water rates
- service charges
- refuse
- bank charges
- accountants
- legal
- cars
- private health
- shoots and shows (photographic work and artistic team projects)
- marketing
- pensions.

MANAGING YOUR CASH-BOOK

Whatever columns you decide upon to list your expenditure, keep them in the same place all the time. This will mean you can easily go back through and add up weekly, monthly and annual turnover and instantly find your information. Create formulae on spreadsheet cells so totals are compiled automatically. These same figures, broken down, will form the basis of your **P&L**.

At the end of every trading week, add up the weekly totals. From this, you can then tot up the monthly (or period), quarterly (three-monthly), biannual (six-monthly) and annual turnover. Use different colours for each so you can see clearly the definition between them. You can add these up on both sides of your cash-book quite easily – income and expenses. These figures, once netted down (where VAT has been taken off), become the basis of your analysis sheets to record where your turnover has come from. Your expenditure will transfer straight to your profit and loss sheet, then go on to form the basis for your financial statements (prepared by your accountant or book-keeper).

From your turnover, it is then relatively simple to calculate and save your VAT from your total salon turnover, and deduct what you will be reclaiming. This will give you an accurate guide of what to save and what you will be liable for when you complete your VAT returns.

Whatever method you use, you need to log these simple payments. I duplicate my cash-book records using software systems to back up my data. Some salon owners will simply want to do things manually, others will choose to do everything on computer and some, like me, will do both. Simply do what works best for you and the person who is looking at your accounts, as you will both need to be able to find a system that you understand and can give you clear information.

DAILY BALANCE

I have always used sticky notes stuck into my cash-book, or balance boxes on my spreadsheets, to keep a record of my current account balance on a day-to-day basis, rather than waiting for the books to be balanced at the end of the week. I can then see at a glance what has been transferred to other accounts, and check their balances, as well as what my current account balance is. This gives me a detailed analysis on which to base my financial decisions.

P&L
Profit and loss account – detailing the income and expenditure by time period (usually monthly) which demonstrates net profit.

Use an old-fashioned adding machine with paper till rolls to refer back to your calculations and spot any mistakes.

Keeping data accurately and up to date is vital if you want to be able to act quickly on any overspending or underperformance.

Remember which money is yours and which belongs to the government. As mentioned in Book 1, all your forecasts must work on your net figures, not your gross. There is no point complaining about the payments you have to make to HMRC – just remember to allow for them!

Transfer your liabilities into the other bank accounts you have created for your savings (see Book 1) on a weekly basis, so as not to confuse your cash flow and think you have more money sitting in your current account than is actually yours! Create several accounts to save for your essential or substantial outgoings – VAT, corporation tax, payroll, rent, etc and even profit – so that your current account acts as your 'purse' or 'wallet' and you do not overspend or get a false picture of your finances.

BANK RECONCILIATION

This is the essential process of balancing up what you should have left with what you have in the bank, bearing in mind what payments out or credits in have yet to clear, and what sums in are in cleared funds. EPOS payments by BACS need to be logged and tracked to ensure they have cleared. You can reconcile your cash-book to your bank statement when it arrives, or you can choose to opt for monthly statements. I tend to reconcile my bank statement to my cash-book at the end of every month or accounting period and, with online banking, you can opt to get a statement to match the exact dates you are reconciling from and to. Whatever way you decide to do this, you must do it regularly (at least monthly), so at the end of your financial year your accounting is relatively straightforward.

IF IT DOES NOT BALANCE

If your cash-book is not reconciling to the balance on your bank statement, list the following:
- cheques issued that have not cleared yet
- credit card payments recorded that have not cleared
- credit card refunds that have led to totals being incorrect
- standing orders that have not gone out or gone out early
- direct debits that have not gone out or gone out early
- number dyslexia by you or the bank – so £10.52 is logged as £10.25
- transfers that have not gone through correctly
- mistakes in your cash-book – totals that are incorrect
- ensure breakdowns in your cash-book tally correctly, ie net and VAT breakdowns of the outgoings.

Do not forget to reconcile your other accounts too, to check that transfers for savings and large liabilities have been done correctly, and match your account/cash-book sums.

YOUR RESPONSIBILITIES

If your name is above the door or on the company registration, whether you are a company director, a sole trader or in partnership, you will be liable and responsible for making sure that records are kept up to date, properly, accurately and for the required length of time (six years at present). You will need to keep paper records like invoices, statements, bills, client receipts, and so on, to verify your audit trail. If you are a salon manager, you may be in charge of keeping on top of these responsibilities for the salon owner.

Even if you delegate this book-keeping task, ultimately it is your responsibility and HMRC will pay short shrift to any lack of accountability. If you are running or managing a salon for someone else, you will still have to get to grips with understanding the book-keeping so you can track your financial success. Sometimes people in our industry are not so keen to do the paperwork, but we cannot manage the bigger picture unless we focus on the detail.

HMRC VISITS

If you have a visit from HMRC, whether they are looking at VAT payments, National Insurance Contributions (NICs) or any other element of your book-keeping, they will want to see an **audit trail**.

Audit trail

This is a paper trail, or computer trail, which records in chronological order the details of every transaction listed/posted to the system.

For instance, imagine you turned over £10 on a particular date, which meant you turned over £1000 in a particular week, and £6000 in a particular month. Where did that initial £10 come from? You will have to show the records that make up that money – the transactions, the client visits, etc. It is the same for expenses and products: you will have to show copies of any payments that were made so a trail can be followed which clearly lists and demonstrates the chain of transactions.

There is no standard timeline for how often you will be visited by the Revenue to inspect both VAT and NICs, but it is usual to expect a visit every five years or so. You will be given notice and are expected to be compliant and accommodating regarding appointments. You are also required to provide all relevant information and have it to hand. If books and records are in storage you will have to get them out ready for the visit.

OTHER ACCOUNTING BOOKS TO KEEP

There are other books (ledgers) that may help you come up with management accounts. The more detailed your in-salon accounting system is, the less work your accountant will have to do at the end of the year; so it makes sense to set up some good accounting practice from the start.

Think about recording the following aspects by keeping:
• invoices received ledger or purchase ledger (invoices issued to you by due date and payment date)
• daily figure book (see Chapter 2)
• invoices issued ledger (for payments into your business
• business card (company credit card) expenses ledger
• stock taking ledger (to accurately calculate your stock holding and stock usage – see Chapter 11)
• bank transfer ledger (for payments to and from your different accounts)
• bank statements folders (to show credits received and payments cashed)
• payroll payments folders (you need to keep records of payments to your employees*).

*Larger businesses will probably employ someone to calculate their payroll expenses if they have lots of employees and staff. Smaller businesses may calculate payments themselves or use an administrative assistant to help them. Working out wages and salaries for your team is complex and requires a real understanding of tax codes, etc. We will look at this in more detail in Chapter 8.

Invoice ledger

Balance outstanding: £1,116.65

Date invoice received	Date order placed	Tax invoice date	Account number	Invoice number	Company name	Category	Details	Net amount	VAT amount	Total amount	Credit note net	Credit note VAT	Credit note total	Revised total	Paid total	VAT reclaimed period	Cheque number	Due date	Paid date	Date of chq clearance
5.1.12	3.1.12	3.1.12	76581	112354	**Viking**	Tel and stat	Stationery	£48.65	£9.73	£58.38	£8.32	£1.66	£9.98	£48.40	£48.40	£48.40	1510	3.2.12	1.2.12	7.2.12
6.1.12	4.1.12	4.1.12	000234568	85426	**L'Oréal**	Purchases	General stock	£650.52	£130.10	£780.62		£0.00	£0.00	£780.62	£780.62		1511	4.2.12	1.2.12	7.2.12
8.1.12	1.1.12–31.1.12	6.1.12	HW987	1423	**Salon PR**	Adv and PR	PR	£140.00	£28.00	£168.00		£0.00	£0.00	£168.00	£168.00	£168.00	1512	6.2.12	1.2.12	8.2.12
15.1.12	1.2.12–30.4.12	15.1.12	H956	19465	**PH Media**	Tel and stat	On hold music	£95.00	£19.00	£114.00		£0.00	£0.00	£114.00	£114.00			15.2.12		
22.1.12	20.1.12	20.1.12	45632	8585	**Essentials**	Purchases	General stock	£83.33	£16.67	£100.00		£0.00	£0.00	£100.00	£100.00			20.2.12		
1.2.12	28.1.12	1.2.12		176	**Glass Care**	Repairs	Repair to mirror	£62.50	£12.50	£75.00		£0.00	£0.00	£75.00	£75.00			14.2.12		
2.2.12	4.2.12	4.2.12	000234568	85956	**L'Oréal**	Purchases	General stock	£523.85	£104.77	£628.62		£0.00	£0.00	£628.62	£628.62			4.3.12		
3.2.12	2.2.12	2.2.12		6238	**Wella**	Purchases	General stock	£165.86	£33.17	£199.03		£0.00	£0.00	£199.03	£199.03			2.3.12		

Business card

Outstanding balance £82.00

Date	Company name	Description	Category	Net amount	VAT	Total	Amount paid	Paid	Card no	VAT reclaimed?	Date paid
30.12.11	**Rymans**	Stationery	Tel and stat	£12.50	£2.50	£15.00	£15.00	✓	3012	✓	28.1.12
1.1.12	**Boots**	Cosmetics	Purchases	£8.33	£1.67	£10.00	£10.00	✓	3012		28.1.12
10.1.12	**Sainsburys**	Refuse sacks	Refuse	£1.84	£0.37	£2.21	£2.21	✓	3012		28.1.12
14.1.12	**Pizza Express**	Entertaining	Sundry	£25.00	£5.00	£30.00	£30.00	✓	3012		28.1.12
18.1.12	**Starbucks**	Entertaining	Sundry	£7.00	£1.40	£8.40	£8.40	✓	3012		28.1.12
20.1.12	**The Florists**	Flowers for reception	Sundry	£20.83	£4.17	£25.00	£25.00	✓	3012		28.1.12
22.1.12	**Turners Garage**	Company car MOT	Cars	£46.67	£9.33	£56.00	£56.00	✓	3012		28.1.12
23.1.12	**Sainsburys**	Magazines	Sundry	£10.00	£2.00	£12.00	£12.00		3012		
26.1.12	**John Lewis**	Lamp for reception	Purchases	£25.00	£5.00	£30.00	£30.00		3012		
2.2.12	**John Lewis**	Light bulbs	Light and heat	£10.83	£2.17	£13.00	£13.00		3012		
2.2.12	**M&A Hygiene**	Toilet roll	Laundry and cleaning	£12.50	£2.50	£15.00	£15.00		3012		
5.2.12	**Marks & Spencer**	Handwash	Laundry and cleaning	£10.00	£2.00	£12.00	£12.00		3012		

View online or download at www.cityandguilds.com/USM

INVOICE LEDGER

You will see in this example that there are several columns to keep:
- date invoice received
- date order placed
- tax invoice date (the date of posting for the supplier)
- account number
- invoice number
- supplier or company name
- category where listed (account/cash-book and P&L)
- details of the order – such as stationery, renewal, etc, for your own reference
- net amount
- VAT amount
- total amount
- credit note net *
- credit note VAT *
- credit note gross*
  *if applicable, but if any credit notes are issued you will need to balance them against the order to which they refer
- revised total (if applicable, after the credit note has been deducted)
- paid total (for completion once the amount is paid)
- VAT reclaimed (for compiling your VAT returns, this tick list will confirm on which VAT return – 1, 2, 3 or 4 – this has been accounted)
- cheque number
- due date (usually 30 days after tax invoice date – see invoice terms)
- paid date (date transaction was posted in account/cash-book)
- date of cheque clearance (for your bank reconciliation)
- balance outstanding – this box can be kept up to date so you have a running total of the amounts outstanding.

BUSINESS CARD EXPENSES LEDGER

You may be issued with a company credit card by your bank, in which case you need to keep a ledger. In this ledger, you need to keep the following columns, which will be entered into your cash-book on the date that the bank deduct the amount from your current account. Therefore, for accurate accounting, you will need to apportion the various expenses into the right columns. Keeping a ledger will help you to categorise these amounts properly.

You should list:

- date of expense
- company name of where card was used
- description of the expense
- category where expense should be entered (in account/cash-book)
- net amount
- VAT
- total
- amount paid
- card number (if more than one director has a company credit card)
- VAT reclaim tick box as per above (and number of return reclaimed on, ie period 1, 2, 3 or 4 – returns are quarterly)
- date paid, ie date the card statement amount was debited from the current account.

PREPARING YOUR VAT RETURNS

You will need to calculate, using your invoice book and account book, the VAT payable from the dates of returns. You can take the majority of your VAT liabilities straight from your account/cash-book and analysis sheets.

To help you calculate the liability, make sure you track plus or minus dates and tax invoice dates.

PLUS OR MINUS DATES

VAT returns are strictly tracked in calendar periods, such as 1 March to 30 June. This will not necessarily fall in line with your fiscal accounting periods, so you will invariably have to add or subtract dates from your week or period end to get the right information from your account/cash-book, both at the beginning of the return date and at the end. I call these 'plus or minus dates'.

TAX INVOICE DATES

Your account/cash-book will list invoices that relate to the period in which they were paid. But for VAT purposes you will need to add and subtract invoices by their tax invoice date – not the date they were paid. At the beginning of the period, you will therefore have to allow for invoices from your last return that you reclaimed VAT on, even though you had not paid them (as by now they have been paid through your account/cash-book); then you will also have to add on invoices that have been issued but not yet paid, if their tax invoice dates fall in line with the VAT return dates. Once you get a pattern established, you will easily be able to deduct one amount at the front end of your workings, and add another amount at the bottom, then carry that amount forward to your next return.

Once you have worked out the above, simply calculate the VAT due on your sales and deduct the VAT you are claiming back (as per above) to work out your final liability.

CONTINUITY IN YOUR BOOK-KEEPING

Whatever books you decide to keep – whether manually or by spreadsheet – it is a good idea to keep your columns and wording itemised as per your account/cash-book, as the information from it will translate directly to the P&L. Variations or different methods of categorising may just give you more work, so try and keep a cohesion between the books you keep.

ACCOUNTING DOS AND DON'TS

Make sure you follow these vital do's and don'ts when it comes to your accounting.

Do:
- keep your records for the required time period (if space is tight it may be necessary to find additional storage); use clear storage boxes that can stack on top of each other and make sure they are well labelled
- ensure you are monitoring, recording, filing and storing all the elements of your audit trail
- find the accounting methods that you understand and work for your business in conjunction with your book-keeper and accountant; if you don't understand, ask
- remember the old adage, 'look after the pennies and the pounds will look after themselves'
- feel free to use manual or software systems – there is no 'correct' way to obtain the right information, do what works best for you, and combine both if you prefer.

Don't:
- just look at the bigger picture, but remember to focus on the daily and weekly situation as a matter of course
- hand your accountant a pile of receipts in a shoe box every six months; rather than ignoring your accounts, get some good systems established then get to grips with your finances every day to make your systems manageable and keep your data accurate.

SUMMARY

It may be tempting to delegate the task, but it is essential to have a thorough understanding of your book-keeping and tracking and to monitor what is being spent, to maximise your profitability. Even if someone is doing this for you, make sure you take time to monitor it regularly to look for trends and patterns.

Get into the regular habit of doing your accounts or getting your cash-book filled in every day so that you can keep on top of controlling your costs; there is no substitute for doing it yourself if you really want to get on top of the finances. Spending a few minutes every day will make your accounting easier and quicker in the long run.

By inputting the information yourself – or at least looking at it regularly – you will easily spot areas of overspending or unnecessary extravagances and so help with your profitability.

CHAPTER 8
FIXED AND VARIABLE COSTS

In this chapter we will look at the two different types of costs that businesses have: fixed and variable. We will learn to differentiate between the two and see how you can make impacts and savings. We will look at the importance of constantly re-evaluating costs, and how frequent negotiation can positively impact your profitability.

FIXED COSTS

Fixed costs are the ones that do not vary with sales – they are harder to change and predetermined. For example, you will pay the same for rent and insurance, no matter how much business you do. **Fixed costs** include:

- rent
- rates – business and water
- insurance premiums
- bank loans
- refuse charges
- service charges
- heat and light
- bank charges
- franchise royalty fees (as a percentage they can vary, but the rate is usually fixed).

VARIABLE COSTS

Variable costs are ones that can vary with sales – they fluctuate and can depend on turnover. For example, you will spend more on laundering towels if you have more customers. **Variable costs** include:

- payroll
- stock purchases
- credit card commission rates
- advertising and PR
- laundry and cleaning
- telephone and stationery
- sundry costs
- repairs and renewals
- accountants' charges
- legal fees
- cars
- private health
- shoots and shows (photographic work, etc)
- marketing
- pensions.

BUDGETING

BUDGETING FOR FIXED COSTS

Although some fixed costs can fluctuate, for example insurance premiums can go up and down, or you can change suppliers for electricity, most fixed costs are quite regular and cannot really be impacted upon. Your local refuse bill, for example, will be what it is and there will be no room for negotiation or manoeuvre on the price. Rates, again, will be set by the council and, although you can appeal (see Book 1), once the decision is made, there is no leeway. Fixed costs have to be met – all your financial planning needs to be designed to be able to carry these expenses. When formulating your business plan, it is vital to make sure these fixed costs are budgeted for and your target turnover can reach them.

BUDGETING FOR VARIABLE COSTS

Variable costs have much more room for manoeuvre. Your telephone bill, for instance, can be reduced by making fewer calls or by changing your service provider and getting a better deal. Some variable costs will automatically increase in line with the business; for instance as you turn over more money you will need to employ more staff and your payroll costs will rise. Variable costs are harder to estimate; it is more likely that you will find out most of these as you go along.

IMPACTING COSTS

HOW TO IMPACT YOUR FIXED COSTS

Although it is harder, you still can evaluate your fixed costs as a regular exercise to look at your spending.

Rent
We covered in Book 1 how to negotiate with your landlord, but your rent will probably be your second biggest expense (after your payroll bill) so it is always worth revisiting the chances of maintaining the rent (if it is subject to review) or negotiating new terms.

Rates
Business rates can be appealed against (see Book 1) but, in all likelihood, you will need to cover this other significant expense and to impact upon it may be litigious, lengthy and time-consuming. Water may be metered, so water rates can vary slightly, but the charges are normally fixed.

Insurance premiums

It is never worth underinsuring. Again, in Book 1, we covered how vital the right level of cover is to give you peace of mind. Increases in premiums will be largely out of your control, but it is worth getting quotes to see if you can renegotiate premiums upon renewal.

Bank loans

If you are borrowing money, this will be a significant cost and will probably not fall liable for renewal very often. Do try to renegotiate your terms with your bank manager, particularly if you can demonstrate some good sets of audited accounts since initial terms were agreed.

Refuse charges

Refuse collection may be subcontracted by your local authority, and possibly will be chargeable by the bag, but there will be little option but to accept your charges.

Service charges

If you are in a mall or complex, service charges will be frustratingly out of your control. They may even go over budget and your careful estimating will be fruitless. They are very often invoiced in arrears, so be sure to allow for this in your cash flow.

Heat and light

Changing energy provider is an option, but gas and electricity prices are largely out of our control and subject to regulation by independent authorities.

Bank charges

Again, thinking about changing banks is an option and it is always worth asking your relationship manager for a different tariff; but on the whole, charges are set and predetermined by the levels of business and turnover you are doing, so there may not be room for manoeuvre.

As you can see from the above, making inroads into your fixed costs is very difficult. Turnover has to be able to meet these expenses, and cash flow has to be able to cover them. Making sure you can pay the fixed cost bills is as vital as ensuring your VAT and Inland Revenue costs are covered, as there is very little you can do to alter them.

HOW TO IMPACT YOUR VARIABLE COSTS

However, there is more control over variable costs. They will need constant evaluation and you can really make some changes which together can have a great impact on your **bottom line**.

Payroll

This is our largest salon expense and, as such, needs constant evaluation. It is essential to track our gross or total payroll (inclusive of payments to HMRC and NICs) as a percentage of our total net (less VAT) turnover at every pay period. It is then a good idea to work out what proportion your nonproductive staff (receptionists, trainees, etc) are of the total payroll cost, and what proportion your productive staff (turnover-producing operators) are, too. I then like to break it down by individual, so that I can get a true picture of each operator's profitability. If turnover is down overall, you need to be looking at the individual productivity of each operator, and whether you can reduce the number of unproductive staff you employ.

The percentage payroll cost you carry will directly impact your profitability, as it is your single biggest expense. But your payroll costs will fluctuate month by month and vary slightly, so do not do anything rash until you can see patterns emerging which suggest you should make some changes. If you are providing top premium service levels and pitching at the higher price end, you will need more unproductive staff in order to provide the service. If you are going for the mass-market, you will need slightly less, and if you are going for the no-frills, competing on price sector, the amount of unproductive staff you employ will be lower still.

What your payroll costs should be

We will look at individual performance later, but as a guide, you should always look at your overall payroll costs (inclusive – not your net or take home pay) as a percentage of your net turnover (after VAT). The benchmark will be between 40% and 60% of your turnover, on average. High end salons will probably even run at 62-65%, bearing in mind we are a service industry. Think of expensive luxury hotels or cruises where the staff to customer ratio is almost 2:1; if we are aiming at these service levels, we cannot cut costs on our staffing levels.

> **Bottom line**
>
> The actual amount of profit, after all costs and deductions have been made (the bottom line on the profit and loss sheet).

So, if we take our fictional salon's turnover as an example:

Gross weekly takings £8000   net weekly takings   £6,666.67
(after VAT at 20%)

Gross payroll @ 55% of net turnover = £3,666.67 per week.

This will be the budget for the entire salaries, including the owner or manager's basic salary (not including dividends), and inclusive of HMRC liabilities and NICs.

In order to work out the monthly figure, we merely multiply the turnover by 52 and divide by 12 (12 monthly pay periods), if we are running our fiscal accounting in this way.

For example: annual net turnover £6,666.67 x 52 =
£346,666.84 divided by 12 = £28,888.90 per month

Note: if this turnover decreases, so must the amount spent on payroll, to keep percentages in line. If turnover increases, the payroll budget will be higher.

Nobody ever won a prize for having the lowest payroll bill. Salons often tell me they are running at 30% for instance, and expect me to be impressed; I'm not! Because often, in the next breath, they are asking me why they cannot retain their staff or saying that their existing client ratio is too low and they cannot sustain repeat business.

You will need to pay people well in order to retain them and get a better grade of operator, but much will depend on where you are pitching your pricing and the service levels you are aiming to offer. However, carefully calculate the following each month to ensure your costs are in line:

1   The percentage of nonproductive staff and their salaries as a percentage of the overall payroll bill
2   The percentage of gross salary to net turnover of each productive operator (which we will cover in more detail later).

Payroll Analysis

Name	Days worked	ROTA	Net takings (inc retail)	Gross pay	%	Av. Net taking/day
Technical						
Taylor	20	20	£11,330.22	£4,690.38	41.4%	£566.51
David	19	20	£13,280.65	£5,530.72	41.6%	£698.98
Marcos	20	20	£11,086.87	£4,486.22	40.5%	£554.34
Kathy	19	20	£9,568.69	£3,802.99	39.7%	£503.62
Samantha	19	20	£9,153.13	£3,619.45	39.5%	£481.74
Adam	18	20	£8,793.04	£3,694.09	42.0%	£488.50
Lauren	19	20	£7,755.87	£3,136.64	40.4%	£408.20
Sally	15	20	£4,967.35	£2,254.13	45.4%	£331.16
Hair						
Nancy	18	20	£17,940.91	£8,856.16	49.4%	£996.72
Harry	19	20	£6,660.22	£2,646.26	39.7%	£350.54
Patrick	21	20	£12,143.43	£5,074.69	41.8%	£578.26
Caron	21	20	£12,869.37	£5,794.71	45.0%	£612.83
Freddie	20	20	£9,951.52	£4,088.88	41.1%	£497.58
Karla	15	20	£5,751.25	£2,168.65	37.7%	£383.42
Billy	20	20	£7,531.39	£2,974.24	39.5%	£376.57
Amanda	18	20	£5,969.57	£2,405.85	40.3%	£331.64
Jason	20	20	£7,311.51	£2,868.03	39.2%	£365.57
Manicure						
Alice	16	16	£2,346.59	£1,047.36	44.6%	£146.66
Emma	6	8	£1,266.52	£622.53	49.2%	£211.09

View online or download at www.cityandguilds.com/USM

Stock purchases

The second biggest change we can make concerns stock spending. As a rule of thumb, between 8 and 12% of our net turnover should be spent on purchasing our stock to use and retail in the salon. I always aim for a straight 10% to make things simple.

When we are looking to introduce treatments and services, we therefore need to work out how much in bulk or professional product it costs to conduct the service. When we are looking at opening orders or increasing the SKUs (stock-keeping units) in an existing range, we also need to be aware of the impact of this financial decision on our stock costs.

There will be a natural proportion of shrinkage and loss with stock – products will go missing or get stolen, professional stock will get overused, staff will use products to carry out complimentary services on each other, stock will be needed for training, etc. It is futile to think this will not happen; it will. But our 10% guideline has to include this fact, and we will look at stock control methods and stocktaking later.

Payroll and stock costs in other retail businesses

Interestingly, other retail businesses find their stock and payroll costs are the other way round. For example in fashion retailing, between 50% and 60% of net turnover is spent on buying stock, whereas they need fewer staff in order to sell the goods, so their payroll bill will be approximately 10%. However, hair and beauty are labour intensive, so our staffing costs will always be the highest expense; but we cannot produce turnover in our sector without our team.

Credit card commission rates

As detailed in Book 1, one of the most productive and easiest ways to make a real impact on your bottom line is to review and shop around for better deals on your EPOS trading. Get detailed figures of how many people are paying by card in percentage terms, track it against last year, look at the value of the turnover going through your EPOS terminals, and tout around for the best deal. Even making a 0.5% difference in your rates will have a massive impact if the vast majority of your clients are paying by card, with no effort (other than some tough negotiating) on your part. Review it every 6–12 months – do not forget, maybe even put it in your diary, as it will seem like yesterday since you looked at it!

Advertising and PR

Perhaps the most insecure of our variable costs, advertising and PR are normally the first to go if profitability is suffering. In harsh economic times, they are often considered a luxury that can ill be afforded if we are struggling to pay other bills.

Laundry and cleaning

Try employing smaller companies rather than larger cleaning contractors, or even think about employing somebody on an individual basis to clean the salon. In tough times, bosses should get their hands dirty (we cleaned our salon for the first five years) so see if cleaning duties can be shared out among the team if funds do not allow for professionals.

Telephone and stationery

You can see if changing service providers will help with your communication costs. You will need a broadband connection and incoming and outgoing lines in your salon, so see if you can negotiate packages with other companies.

Sundry costs

Sundry costs can easily add up – a pack of plasters here, some sticky-tack and pencils there, taxis, entertaining, and so on. But you can make some real inroads into reducing your spend just through monitoring what you are spending on sundry costs yourself and looking back to ensure wastage is minimal. However, be sure you do not cut back on costs which impact on the client experience. Frayed towels, tatty gowns, etc, are not acceptable in today's competitive market. Track your spending on the small stuff so you can splash out on the things the clients notice – like fresh flowers on the desk and up-to-date magazines.

Repairs and renewals

Maintenance is essential – a well maintained salon is absolutely critical, whatever level you are pitching at. Do not scrimp on client-associated costs like repairs – chipped paint, broken tiles, missing chair feet, broken trolleys or backwashes that do not work. These will all get noticed by the customer, so make sure you tell your staff to inform you of anything that needs attention immediately and never be afraid to pay up and sort it out at once.

Accountant's charges

You can shop around here – but what you pay your accountant will largely depend on the level of services you need them to perform for you. For instance, they may be calculating your monthly payroll bill dependent on the figures you are providing to them (individual turnover, attendance records, vacation records, etc) or working out your self-assessment tax; they may merely be doing your annual audited accounts. Speak to your accountant about ways in which costs could be reduced, and let them know if you are finding it hard to pay their fees – they may be willing to cut their services and limit their time or agree new working practices in order to keep you as a customer.

Legal fees

Nobody knows what will come up legally or when and why you will need to cover legal fees – an employment dispute, action by a disgruntled customer, etc – none can be really budgeted for. Some legal cover may be provided under your insurance premium, so check. Lawyers are notoriously expensive, so be aware of costs before picking up the phone.

Cars

Frequent budgetary changes mean that company cars can sometimes be tax-efficient, and sometimes the opposite – a burdensome cost. Which employees, if any, are allowed the perk and privilege of a car is a discretionary matter. It may be only the salon owner or manager, if at all, who is allowed a company vehicle. Whoever gets one, there are ongoing costs to consider – petrol, road tax, servicing, MOT and insurance are all related costs. You also have to consider how the car is financed in the first place (bought outright, lease purchase, etc). See Chapter 7 on asset management in Book 1.

Private healthcare

Offering private healthcare to selected employees is a salary bonus that may be necessary to consider. Rates are dependent on age and can be negotiable, but will only ever increase based on the undisputed fact that the employee will be getting older. It may be a privilege too far in tough economic times, and a contribution from the employee concerned may be requested or required if it is considered crucial to their salary package.

Shoots and shows (photographic work, etc)

You need to be very clear on how the salon can benefit from the cost of being involved with shows or producing photographic work – the chances of creative work benefitting the bottom line profit is minimal. Be sure to set firm budgets and make certain that all costs are calculated within them – model rights (the right to use or publish the resulting work) can be costly and studio time is never cheap, so ensure the team member responsible has clear and succinct guidelines and budgets to follow.

Marketing

Marketing can be expensive but may be crucial in helping with the client numbers. You must be sure to evaluate carefully what is working and proving effective, and what is not bringing the customers in. Try to get suppliers to help with the cost of in-salon marketing, and dual brand incentives and promotions so there is a tangible benefit to them, too.

Pensions

If you have more than five employees you are obligated to run a stakeholder pension scheme, but as yet employers are not obliged to contribute. However, company pension schemes are different and are proving to be a costly way to encourage loyalty and staff retention. Speak to an independent financial advisor to find out whether you should be offering a company pension scheme and, if so, how you can make it more cost effective.

SUMMARY

Do not be reactive; looking at costs needs a proactive stance – learn to anticipate your costs and work on them regularly. You should not act only when your costs are too high or not in line with your forecasts and then have to wait for the changes you make to impact. Time is of the essence.

Little changes, like knocking £300 off your annual laundry bill, might seem inconsequential and hardly worth the hassle, but they will all add up to make greater profitability. Little impacts, wherever possible, will come together to make a big impact, so do not be tempted to ignore the detail, or forget to bother with little savings here and there. Sometimes you can get bogged down in looking for one big answer, where actually small changes can have the required effect.

Get into the habit of really knowing and understanding how your payroll costs are made up – regularly review your percentages to check they are in line and get on top of any issues straight away.

Remember our adage: turnover is vanity, profit is sanity, but cash flow is reality. Your profitability is just as important as, if not more than, important as your turnover, so regularly evaluate your fixed and variable costs and look for little areas of improvement.

CHAPTER 9
CASH FLOW, TURNOVER AND PROFIT

In this chapter we will look at what cash flow means to your business, how to define turnover and what is classed as profit. We will get familiar with some of the terms your accountant uses so you understand the financial jargon and the numbers are demystified. We will analyse what your profit percentages should be, and how to track that you are in line with your financial aims.

CASH FLOW

This is the money that goes into and out of your business current account – the flow of cash into your salon from which all the bills are paid.

Often cash flow is thought of as being the same as turnover, but the cash going into your business need not necessarily come from takings; it could also be regular inputs of money from investors, or any other such income – hence you hear the term 'cash flow injection'. A business can survive without making a profit, but it cannot survive without cash flow. Think of your cash flow as the blood flowing round the veins of the body of your business.

A cash flow statement is merely a summary of where the cash into the business has come from and gone to. Your cash-book or account book will provide you with a summary of cash flow and give you an adequate statement if kept accurately and up to date.

TURNOVER

Gross turnover

Before VAT has been deducted.

Net turnover

After VAT has been deducted.

Turnover is the money that comes into your salon till, the money that is generated from sales – your takings. Turnover is what we should always be looking to increase. You can talk in terms of **gross turnover** or **net turnover**.

For management accounting purposes, always talk in terms of net turnover. Working with the figures after VAT due has been taken off will give you a true picture of your finances. Remember that the VAT element does not belong to us, so what comes into our tills does not truly belong to us either until the VAT has been deducted. Working in gross never gives you a true picture, although gross figures are what our teams and operators tend to understand when it comes to their individual performance.

PROFIT

This is the money left over, after all your expenses have been paid. There are two ways of looking at profit: you can either look at **gross profit** or **net profit**. You may also come across the terms **pretax profits** or **profit margin**.

GROSS PROFIT

Gross profit is a calculation which some accountants use it and tends to be more relevant in other sectors; for instance in catering, where the cost of goods is a vital calculation for getting correct food and beverage per head ratios. It is also sometimes used for insurance purposes to calculate what levels of cover would be needed, for example, if you were unable to trade. Gross profit percentages will be between 45% and 60%, but this statistic can often be interpreted in different ways; so do not worry too much if your gross profit differs – it is the net profit that matters. For accounting purposes in our sector, it is a pretty meaningless statistic and one which can be interpreted in various ways. Net profit is the figure you need to understand in order to maximise your profitability.

NET PROFIT

This is your bottom line profit – the final and absolute figure by which you can calculate your profitability. Net profit, like gross profit, can be shown both as a total figure in pounds and as a percentage of net turnover. Net profit is before corporation tax is paid (if applicable), but this will always be paid nine months after the year end period and, if you are wise, you will estimate it and save for it as you go.

HOW PROFITABLE SHOULD YOU BE?

As a guideline, most businesses look for 10% net profit once they are successfully established, regardless of the sector or industry. If you are reinvesting in your brand by keeping it well maintained and looked after, and thinking about long-term goals, you will be hard pushed to be more profitable than this. Some businesses run between 5% and 20% net profit but I tend to find that if you are looking to develop and cultivate your brand in the long term, more than 10% profitability is harder to achieve.

Gross profit

The figure from which the cost of producing the sales has been deducted, so net turnover less what it cost to produce the sales (payroll, stock).

Net profit

Total sales revenue minus all costs (variable costs and fixed costs).

Pretax profits

Net profits before taxes (like corporation tax for limited companies) are paid.

Profit margin

The margin (distance) between making a profit and not, often expressed as a percentage, ie the business has a 5% net profit margin.

If you want to look at your finances in the simplest possible terms, think about your net turnover less your total expenses = either profit or loss.

However other sectors may make up their percentage expenditure, for instance in my previous example of the retail sector, the 10% net profit golden rule pretty much applies across the board. If you hear people talking of 30% or 40% profit margins, you are sure to find they are referring to gross profit and getting confused between the two. More than 10% net profit may be overambitious, and if the rule works for companies like Virgin which run anything from record companies to trains, it can work for us, too.

Some companies which brag about their profitability are normally failing to reinvest properly or are not paying people well enough, so do not be swayed by what other people tell you. Do what works for you.

TO SHOW OR NOT TO SHOW?

Do not expect to make 10% net profit in your first or even second trading year. Have realistic expectations. Remember, a business can survive without making profit – as long as it is paying its staff, liabilities and expenses. Profit is a luxury, not a necessity, when you first start out.

Of course, the way you run your business and what you decide to spend is up to you. If, as the owner or manager, you are paying yourself as part of the payroll, you can decide to reward yourself very well financially and this will increase your wage costs dramatically, affecting your bottom line. You can, alternatively pay yourself a low salary and show more profitability and reward yourself with dividends or bonuses at the end of your financial year. There will be tax implications for showing more company profitability but these have to be mitigated against any personal tax liabilities – so take both into consideration.

Showing as much profit as possible will make your company more saleable, as value is calculated on a multiple of the profits, as previously mentioned, which is calculated using the Price Earnings Ratio (the share price divided by earnings per share). Showing less profit will make your bottom line less desirable and therefore your company will not be worth as much. However, this will only be relevant to your long-term exit plans, if you have any. Sometimes, companies that are gearing up for sale ensure they look as profitable as possible for as many sets of audited accounts as necessary. If you are not planning to sell your company or have it valued for any reason, you will still want it to be as profitable as possible but it will not be critical to its value. However, if you want to increase any borrowings, you will need to ensure your company accounts look as healthy as possible to show the bank manager or potential investors that the business is profitable.

MANAGING YOUR CASH FLOW

Cash flow coming into your current business account can be misleading. It is easy to think there is enough money in your account to make financial decisions, when you may be creating a false picture and you should be saving up for other, larger sums of expenditure that are pending.

Rather like our great-grandparents did, in the days when only the very wealthy had money in the bank, and the rest had to budget carefully and pay their expenses in cash, we should dish out our money and save it appropriately. Before bank accounts, when the weekly wage was brought home in cash, there were often jars across the mantelpiece where the money was distributed into the relevant pots to pay for food, rent, clothes, savings, etc. It is not a bad habit to get into with our cash flow.

Make sure you bank your cash daily. Most clients pay by card these days, so it may be tempting to wait and bank your cash takings at the end of the working week, but regular and daily banking will all help your cash flow situation and make your bank reconciliation easier, too.

MANAGING THE MONEY

We may not have jars across the mantelpiece but we can use our back accounts wisely. Leaving large sums in your regular business current account can confuse you and may make you think you are better off than you actually are.

As mentioned in Chapter 7 of Book 1, you should open several accounts to save for:
- rent – which may be quarterly
- HMRC – VAT, Inland Revenue, NICs
- long-term projects like refurbishment, expansion or nasty impending expenses, like rent hikes
- tax liabilities or corporation tax (do not forget to split this into this year's liabilities and last year's liabilities as your corporation tax bill is payable nine months after year end)
- and, of course, profit! Putting 10% away as you earn it is not a bad idea.

Interest rates may not be great (at the time of writing), but if you are regularly saving money for large bills in separate accounts that you may not need to access frequently, try and negotiate some sort of interest-bearing account for any bank accounts you open for savings and transfers.

Online banking makes it easier to transfer and manage your money and to make sure you can meet large bills when they come in. Think of your business current account rather like your purse – it is where the money comes in and goes out again, but you wouldn't leave a lump sum there and pay your mortgage from it, for instance, so putting the different sums aside will give you a clearer picture.

If you do not manage your cash flow in this way, you can get very confused about how much money you have – and you could make some seriously bad decisions. Clearing it out of your current account and getting it out of the way will make it much easier to judge your financial position.

Regulating cash flow

There will be times when your cash flow may get a bit sticky, and at certain regular periods you may need to dip into your overdraft facility, if applicable, perhaps for pay days. However, if this is happening too often or regularly, you need to get back to your business plan and work out what is going wrong. Maybe your turnover is not what it should be, or your costs are too high and you are overspending. Perhaps you need a cash injection, so refinancing to help you through should be considered.

WHAT TO PAY FROM YOUR CURRENT ACCOUNT DIRECTLY

General bills and expenses can be paid directly from your current business account, rather like (using the purse analogy) buying small day-to-day items like a coffee or bus fare. The type of bills you can get used to paying direct from your current account include:

- small utilities bills – water rates, refuse, etc
- stock – pay little and often to help cash flow
- one-off payments, such as to PRS (for licences to play music in your salons)
- business rates (normally by direct debit)
- bank charges (monthly and normally directly debited from your account)
- insurance premiums (monthly payment instalments can be arranged)
- regular monthly payments like private health cover, PR, cleaning, etc.

WHAT TO SAVE AND TRANSFER

There are several things that you will need to save for and transfer into your current account to pay as required.

VAT

It is important not to fall behind in your VAT payments, and if you are doing accurate accounting you can easily work out what you owe from the week's turnover (by deducting 20% from your turnover) and then deduct the total of VAT you will be claiming back from the payments in the period from your cash-book. You can then transfer the VAT liability directly out of your current business account into a savings account in readiness for the completion of your VAT return, and hopefully earn a bit of interest, too.

Payroll and HMRC

As payroll makes up the biggest expense, and our operators are the generators of our turnover, it makes sense to make sure you can always meet your payroll bill and Inland Revenue expenses. If you find you struggle to meet pay day, get into the habit of transferring regular amounts so that it is never a surprise. Once you have an idea of your monthly payroll costs, transfer a little each week to give you a payment cushion – HMRC do not like to be kept waiting for their money, so you must ensure you can manage the payments.

Rent

Rent payments may be quarterly or monthly, and they may be subject to VAT. As they will invariably be the second largest aspect of your expenditure, it is worth saving up to ensure you can meet the invoice when it arrives. VAT on rent, if charged by your landlord, may be hefty and, although it can be reclaimed, it still needs to be found from your cash flow; so work out how much of your turnover you need to transfer each week. That way, rather than a large chunk of cash flow being taken in one go, you will ease the pain of your rent payments.

Profit

Get into the habit of saving 10% of your net turnover every week. Put this into an instant access account, so you can get at it quickly if you need to. If you regularly save your profit, you can pretty much work out what you have left over and can make decisions on your irregular spending – things that you do not buy very often, such as splashing out on new equipment or on some special advertising.

Tax liabilities or corporation tax

Remember, if you are a sole trader or partnership you will need to save for your tax liabilities and you will need to pay income tax on any profits you make via your self-assessment forms.

If you are a limited company you will need to be saving for your corporation tax too – so as a rough equation, 20% of your estimated net profit will need to be saved for payment of this tax nine months after your financial year end. You will need to keep last year's tax due in a separate account, while you are saving for your current financial year as you go, to be entirely straight.

SUMMARY

It is essential to be familiar with your profitability and understand the terms your accountant uses. However, it need not be complicated. If you are not making enough money, remember there are only two solutions: control your costs or increase your turnover. A little bit of both usually does the trick.

Profit margins are tight in our sector – 10% net profit is the goal, so the difference between making profit and missing it is minimal. Small, regular tweaks can make a big impact. Remember, you cannot manage what you do not monitor – so look at your profitability regularly.

Opening up several different accounts to save for larger items of expenditure will help you budget and save, as well as giving you an essential understanding of where the money is going.

CHAPTER 10
PROFIT AND LOSS

In this chapter, we'll look at how to read and understand a profit and loss (P&L) account, and to turn the information it contains into a chart to help you understand your expenditure and maximise your profitability. We will look at how to track your actual performance against your planned and last year's P&Ls. We will also learn how to create a 'profit circle' pie chart to demonstrate your costs and educate your team and give them a greater understanding of the role they play in the salon's profitability.

Profit and loss

P&L stands for a profit and loss account.

A **profit and loss** (P&L) account details income and expenditure by time period (usually monthly), and demonstrates net profit. Once you have understood what it shows, it is essential to monitor it closely. Now we have defined our profitability, we need to examine ways in which we can monitor and track it.

Profit & Loss

	1	2	3	4	5	6	7	8	9	10	11	12	TOTAL	% Of Sales
INCOME														
suppliers' incentive	£100.00	£100.00	£100.00	£100.00	£100.00	£100.00	£100.00	£100.00	£100.00	£100.00	£100.00	£100.00	£1,200.00	0.00%
miscellaneous	£75.00	£75.00	£75.00	£75.00	£75.00	£75.00	£75.00	£75.00	£75.00	£75.00	£75.00	£75.00	£900.00	
online sales	£100.00	£100.00	£100.00	£100.00	£100.00	£100.00	£100.00	£100.00	£100.00	£100.00	£100.00	£100.00	£1,200.00	
rent received	£100.00	£100.00	£100.00	£100.00	£100.00	£100.00	£100.00	£100.00	£100.00	£100.00	£100.00	£100.00	£1,200.00	
interest	£25.00	£25.00	£25.00	£25.00	£25.00	£25.00	£25.00	£25.00	£25.00	£25.00	£25.00	£25.00	£300.00	
sales	£26,666.67	£26,666.67	£33,333.34	£26,666.67	£26,666.67	£33,333.34	£26,666.67	£26,666.67	£33,333.34	£26,666.67	£26,666.67	£33,333.34	£346,666.72	
TOTAL	£27,066.67	£27,066.67	£33,733.34	£27,066.67	£27,066.67	£33,733.34	£27,066.67	£27,066.67	£33,733.34	£27,066.67	£27,066.67	£33,733.34	£351,466.72	
EXPENDITURE														
dividends/loan	£0.00	£0.00	£0.00	£0.00	£0.00	£0.00	£0.00	£0.00	£0.00	£0.00	£0.00	£0.00	£0.00	0.00%
payroll	£14,666.68	£14,666.68	£18,333.35	£14,666.68	£14,666.68	£18,333.35	£14,666.68	£14,666.68	£18,333.35	£14,666.68	£14,666.68	£18,333.35	£190,666.84	54.25%
purchases	£2,666.66	£2,666.66	£3,333.33	£2,666.66	£2,666.66	£3,333.33	£2,666.66	£2,666.66	£3,333.33	£2,666.66	£2,666.66	£3,333.33	£34,666.60	9.86%
rent	£3,333.32	£3,333.32	£4,166.65	£3,333.32	£3,333.32	£4,166.65	£3,333.32	£3,333.32	£4,166.65	£3,333.32	£3,333.32	£4,166.65	£43,333.16	12.33%
rates	£280.00	£280.00	£350.00	£280.00	£280.00	£350.00	£280.00	£280.00	£350.00	£280.00	£280.00	£350.00	£3,640.00	1.04%
service charge	£160.00	£160.00	£200.00	£160.00	£160.00	£200.00	£160.00	£160.00	£200.00	£160.00	£160.00	£200.00	£2,080.00	0.59%
adv/pr	£250.00	£250.00	£312.50	£250.00	£250.00	£312.50	£250.00	£250.00	£312.50	£250.00	£250.00	£312.50	£3,250.00	0.92%
insurance	£416.66	£416.66	£416.66	£416.66	£416.66	£416.66	£416.66	£416.66	£416.66	£416.66	£416.66	£416.66	£4,999.92	1.42%
laundry/clean	£245.00	£245.00	£306.00	£245.00	£245.00	£306.00	£245.00	£245.00	£306.00	£245.00	£245.00	£306.00	£3,184.00	0.91%
heat/light	£245.00	£245.00	£306.00	£245.00	£245.00	£306.00	£245.00	£245.00	£306.00	£245.00	£245.00	£306.00	£3,184.00	0.91%
tel & stat	£230.00	£230.00	£285.00	£230.00	£230.00	£285.00	£230.00	£230.00	£285.00	£230.00	£230.00	£285.00	£2,980.00	0.85%
refurbish/cap ex	£150.00	£150.00	£187.50	£150.00	£150.00	£187.50	£150.00	£150.00	£187.50	£150.00	£150.00	£187.50	£1,950.00	0.55%
refuse	£145.00	£145.00	£183.00	£145.00	£145.00	£183.00	£145.00	£145.00	£183.00	£145.00	£145.00	£183.00	£1,892.00	0.54%
sundry	£565.00	£565.00	£565.00	£565.00	£565.00	£565.00	£565.00	£565.00	£565.00	£565.00	£565.00	£565.00	£6,780.00	1.93%
repairs	£150.00	£150.00	£190.00	£150.00	£150.00	£190.00	£150.00	£150.00	£190.00	£150.00	£150.00	£190.00	£1,960.00	0.56%
bank charges	£85.00	£85.00	£106.00	£85.00	£85.00	£106.00	£85.00	£85.00	£106.00	£85.00	£85.00	£106.00	£1,104.00	0.31%
accountants	£165.00	£165.00	£206.25	£165.00	£165.00	£206.25	£165.00	£165.00	£206.25	£165.00	£165.00	£206.25	£2,145.00	0.61%
legal	£100.00	£100.00	£150.00	£100.00	£100.00	£150.00	£100.00	£100.00	£150.00	£100.00	£100.00	£150.00	£1,400.00	0.40%
cars	£0.00	£0.00	£0.00	£0.00	£0.00	£0.00	£0.00	£0.00	£0.00	£0.00	£0.00	£0.00	£0.00	0.00%
Health insurance	£0.00	£0.00	£0.00	£0.00	£0.00	£0.00	£0.00	£0.00	£0.00	£0.00	£0.00	£0.00	£0.00	0.00%
shoots/shows	£0.00	£0.00	£0.00	£0.00	£0.00	£0.00	£0.00	£0.00	£0.00	£0.00	£0.00	£0.00	£0.00	0.00%
p.pensions	£0.00	£0.00	£0.00	£0.00	£0.00	£0.00	£0.00	£0.00	£0.00	£0.00	£0.00	£0.00	£0.00	0.00%
credit card comm	£530.00	£530.00	£690.00	£530.00	£530.00	£690.00	£530.00	£530.00	£690.00	£530.00	£530.00	£690.00	£7,000.00	1.99%
TOTAL	£24,383.32	£24,383.32	£30,287.24	£24,383.32	£24,383.32	£30,287.24	£24,383.32	£24,383.32	£30,287.24	£24,383.32	£24,383.32	£30,287.24	£316,215.52	89.97%
PROFIT	£2,683.35	£2,683.35	£3,446.10	£2,683.35	£2,683.35	£3,446.10	£2,683.35	£2,683.35	£3,446.10	£2,683.35	£2,683.35	£3,446.10	£35,251.20	10.03%
% PROFIT	9.91%	9.91%	10.22%	9.91%	9.91%	10.22%	9.91%	9.91%	10.22%	9.91%	9.91%	10.22%	10.03%	10.03%
corporation tax														

HOW TO READ A P&L

In our example salon, we are looking at the P&L of the current business account, through which the salon's income and expenditure is running. You can see along the top row that the periods are split into twelve, with every third period being a five-week 'month' (shown in italics).

INCOME

All income here is shown net of VAT so we can establish accurate turnover and revenue. Hellen's Hair and Beauty Salon shows income from the following sources for each period:
- main salon turnover (sales)
- other income, eg suppliers, retrospective discounts, online sales, rent of any sublet areas, online sales or e-commerce
- interest
- **grand total income**.

It is important to separate out your net income in this manner so you can accurately see the different sources of revenue coming in.

EXPENDITURE

In the same time columns, ie split into the 12 periods, we will now look at all the outgoings, net of VAT, that were entered into the account/cash-book during that period. Fixed and variable costs, as covered in Chapter 8, are all shown here.

All figures (except where* applies – see Exceptions) are derived from the monthly total in your account/cash-books, that has been compiled by simply adding together the number of weeks' column totals to get the period total. If you are running your account/cash-book by spreadsheet, you can create formulae to add the total period/monthly costs up for you.

The different outgoings are as listed below – followed by one for grand total expenditure.

Dividends/loans
Dividends and loans include any loan repayments to company directors or dividends issued. Monthly bank loan payments can also be entered here (directors' salaries should be included in payroll costs).

Payroll
Payroll is the total cost for the period, shown inclusive of all HMRC payments. There are options in calculating this figure.

Purchases
This requires another calculation to get the correct information.

Rent

Rent may be paid quarterly or monthly. Monthly is preferable for cash flow purposes but, if it is due quarterly, remember this will show a peak and trough effect, ie two months of no rent, one month of three months' worth of rent – so do not panic. Remember, rent should be shown net of VAT (if applicable).

Rates

Business and water rates are shown in this column. Remember that business rates are normally calculated to be paid over 10 months (April to February inclusive, usually) so you will get some periods where no business rates are shown at all.

Service charges

If these are applicable, your service charges can come out quarterly or monthly.

PR

PR is usually a monthly fee, but any marketing activities that are not included in stationery spend, such as e-blasts, etc, should be listed here.

Insurance

Insurance premiums are normally calculated to enable you to pay monthly rather than annually.

Laundry & cleaning

This could include some sundry costs associated with laundry/cleaning, for example soap powder, if you do not use a cleaning company.

Heat/light

If payments for heat and light are not included in your service charges, your electricity and gas bills are shown here.

Telephone & stationery

Telephone and stationery costs are listed here. It should also include any relevant equipment purchased as well as charges for broadband.

Refurbishment & capital expenditure

Refurbishment or other capital expenditure – this will be for any sums spent on refitting the salon or buying new equipment, etc.

Refuse

Your local authority monthly charges for rubbish and recycling collections go here.

Sundry

This area includes all general expenses that are not categorised elsewhere, including entertaining costs.

Repairs & renewals

You should list here all general maintenance expenses.

Bank charges

All general monthly account charges should be shown here.

Accountants

Any fees for your accountant or book-keeper should be listed here.

Legal expenses

As and when any legal matters occur, solicitors' and lawyers' fees should be shown here.

Cars

Any company car payments and expenses should be listed here.

Private health cover

You should list here any applicable charges for private health cover for directors or employees.

Shoots & shows

Any expenses for photographic or artistic work are listed here.

Pensions

Any company pension scheme sums paid during the period are shown here, including for a stakeholder pension (if made by the company).

Credit card commission

Any bills for EPOS (electronic point of sale) are listed here.

GRAND TOTAL EXPENDITURE

Other items

Other columns you may want to add could include:

- franchise fees
- PRS/PRL licences (for playing recorded music in your salons) – alternatively you can file these under legal
- Special Treatment Licences – again, could be filed under legal
- your personalised columns from your own account/cash-book.

EXCEPTIONS

*1 As your HMRC bill for a payroll period is payable the month after the pay period, you can either decide to show on your P&L:

a) the net payroll for this period, say period 3, together with the HMRC bill for the previous period 2, which has actually been paid out of your account/cash-book during period 3

or

b) the net payroll for this period 3, and include the payroll bill that relates to period 3, even though the amount will not get paid out through your account/cash-book until the next month, period 4.

Note: b) is the most accurate way to calculate your true payroll costs, but can be a little confusing, as your cash-book will not balance without taking this into account. You can simply remember that for P&L purposes, your HMRC payroll costs will be a month in arrears compared with your account/cash-book; but do not forget this or your figures will not tally.

*2 Again, to get a true and accurate picture of your stock costs, you need to enter here not what you have spent on stock in the period, but what you have used. To do this you need to follow this simple calculation:

Stocktake value at the commencement of the period (counted and added up)
Plus:
Stock purchased during the period (from your account/cash-book)
Minus:
Stock remaining at the end of the period (counted and added up) = **stock usage for the period**.

STOCK TAKING

Use a stocktaking book, listing all the items you buy to use professionally or retail in your salon and stocktake by brand, noting the unit prices next to each item so you can tot up the value of your stockholding. More detail about stocktaking can be found in the next chapter.

You should do this every month and, once you get into the swing of doing these sums, it is relatively easy to do a quick stocktake at the end of the period and tot up the value of the stock you are holding. This figure will then become your starting figure for the following period, so once you start getting in a pattern it is not too difficult. There are software systems that can help you do this.

Alternatively, you can just enter the net purchases figure from your account/cash-book, but it will not be entirely accurate for accounting purposes.

HOW TO USE YOUR P&L

Your P&L is for management accounting purposes – in other words, it is a tool for you to manage your salon finances. Some payments are only made every three months, and will impact in different quarters. Ideally, all payments would be monthly to enable you to get into a regular pattern with your payments and expenditure but, in reality, there will be several payments that will go out annually, biannually or quarterly, which will affect your budgeting. The more you get used to looking at your P&L, the easier you will find it to understand these peaks and troughs. This may mean that, in some periods, your business looks unrealistically profitable and, in other months, you look unprofitable. The end-of-year figures are the ultimate benchmark of your profitability, and compiling the percentage of turnover your expenses relates to will help you budget for the next financial year.

Now you have the grand total of your income, and the grand total of your outgoings, you can simply work out your profit for each period.

Grand total income minus grand total expenditure = net profit

So from our example, we can see that:
£351,466.72 – £316,215.52 = £35,251.20

You can then express this net profit figure as a percentage of your net turnover by:

Total net profit ÷ grand total income, then multiply by 100 = Net profit %

Again, we can see that:
£35,251.20 ÷. £351,466.72, then x100 = 10.03%

You can do this same sum for the grand total of your financial year once all the periods are completed.

If you are doing your P&L on a spreadsheet, you can create formulae to express sums as percentages and also total up your sums as you go along.

Finally, in the last columns, you can see the total of the individual rows that make up the different elements of expenditure for the financial year. These too can be expressed as a percentage of the annual turnover, so you can accurately assess your fixed costs and look at your variables. At the bottom, there is space to calculate your tax liabilities so you can accurately save for them and get no nasty surprises from HMRC.

P&LS TO CREATE

Using these same sheets, you can get a bit creative. You need to have three sets of P&Ls to really track your costs correctly:

1   Set out your **plan P&L** (from your business plan and the targets you have set) so you can compare it against your actual. This will be ongoing so you can then track your actual profitability against your planned figures.
2   Also, save any **last year's P&Ls**, so you can track any differences in both turnover and expenditure.
3   Finally, of course, your **actual P&L** is what you are going to be looking at in any current financial year, and what you will be comparing the plan and the previous year against.

LOOKING AT YOUR P&L

Too many people only look at P&Ls at the end of the financial year, when it is too late to impact on your profitability. By keeping management accounts and entering the data monthly, or at the end of each financial trading period, you will be completely on top of your spending and be able to see at a glance where:

I like to highlight any areas that are falling short in bright yellow, so I can instantly see where things are not in line, both in terms of income and expenditure.

a) your income is not meeting the target figures that you have set yourself and entered into your plan P&L

b) your expenditure is going over your plan P&L sums.

Looking at it in this way will ensure you can take immediate action to mitigate any losses and be on top of any poor performance; benchmarking your actual P&L against your plan P&L and your LY P&L will give you even greater clarity. This kind of financial analysis gives you a huge advantage over less rigorous competitors, and is essential if you want to be a real business success.

PREPARING YOUR PLAN P&L

It is wise to assume your costs will always be a little higher than you think – invariably you will spend more than you budget for and you will go over on your outgoings. You should not expect to make a profit in the first trading year – there will undoubtedly be unforeseen expenses from your initial 'back of a beermat' calculations. Be a realist (or even a pessimist) and underestimate your turnover a little, while overestimating your costs. You can only be pleasantly surprised that way!

BUSINESS PLAN VERSUS P&L

This is a little bit of a 'chicken and egg' scenario, as your business plan is written once you have done your homework and established as much fact on the potential profitability as possible; these figures form the basis of the targets you set. However, once you have a couple of months' trading under your belt, and you have started to compare your actual P&L to your plan P&L, it is inevitable that some discrepancies will arise. You cannot possibly factor in everything on your business plan and be expected to have a comprehensive understanding of your costs and turnover until you are properly up and running. Your plan P&L will naturally evolve each year, as your actual P&L materialises. You may need to rejig some of your target figures once trading is established and fully underway – your P&L is always a 'work progress' and should be treated as such. It gets more interesting and useful when you have a last year (LY) P&L to compare with.

WHAT IF YOUR PLAN P&L DOES NOT SHOW PROFITABILITY?

It is vital to establish your breakeven figure – the minimum amount of net monthly turnover you need to produce to cover the costs that your plan P&L shows. This needs to be the focus for setting or possibly resetting your targets and breaking down who needs to do what in order to achieve this figure. Sometimes, salon owners say to me that their plan works perfectly until they have to pay their VAT – remember, if your plan does not work in net, it does not work at all. Dipping into your VAT to make it work merely demonstrates that the business model is flawed.

ISSUES TO CONSIDER

If your plan is not working, you should look at the following factors.

Variable costs
Fixed costs cannot really be changed but variable costs can be worked on. Look at key areas like stock spend and payroll and see what needs tweaking to make the percentages work.

Turnover
What ideas can you implement to maximise your income? Can you sublet areas (check your lease terms) to introduce new services, like catering or beauty (if you do not already have them), to generate regular rental income?

General expenditure
Saving little amounts here and there will really add up to make a big impact, so spend time going through each cost and see what you can do to decrease your spending.

Sundry costs
So much can get assigned as sundries, so ensure you go through these thoroughly once you are up and running and stamp out any unnecessary spending, such as entertaining. Look for patterns by going back through your account/cash-book to check all the details.

Extravagance
Are you 'cutting your cloth' accordingly? Big ideas and budgets can only become a reality once you are performing well enough to afford them.

Negotiation
See if you can negotiate some better deals – EPOS, bank loans, etc, can all be up for review. So if the plan P&L is not working, start to talk to your suppliers and providers and see what options there are for your terms.

DOS AND DON'TS

Do:

- look at saving on non-essentials – PR, shoots, shows, company cars and private health care are luxuries that only profitable businesses can afford
- make sure your staff have enough stock to offer the right service levels but look at measures to reduce wastage.

Don't:

- scrimp on any costs that the customer could notice – like cleaning, repairs and renewals, staffing, etc – as anything that affects the customer may affect the turnover; saving on new towels and gowns, for instance, is a false economy because the customer can always tell when a salon is cutting the wrong costs.

PROFIT CIRCLE

I love showing my profit as a pie chart, or profit circle, as it demonstrates so clearly where the money goes.

You can create your circle using your computer software chart and graph wizards, or do it by pen and paper once you know the percentages. You can use different colours for each area of expenditure or split the costs into two colours only – one for fixed costs and one for variable – so you can instantly see where you could make savings in your profitability.

The profit circle makes for a really good staff meeting, but not often. Once in a blue moon the staff need to know about your turnover, and it is healthy for them to realise the business needs to be, and is profitable, because it demonstrates financial security; both of the business and for them. However, the financial management is your job; therefore you should do this once in a while so everyone gets a feel for why you budget in the way you do – but do not make it a regular lecture.

The profit circle

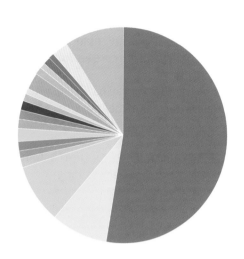

- Profit 10.17%
- Credit card comm 2.02%
- Legal 0.4%
- Accountants 0.62%
- Bank charges 0.32%
- Repairs 0.57%
- Sundry 1.96%
- Refuse 0.55%
- Refurbish/cap ex 0.56%
- Tel and stat 0.86%
- Heat/light 0.92%
- Laundry/clean 0.92%
- Insurance 1.44%
- Pr 0.94%
- Service charge 0.60%
- Rates 1.05%
- Rent 12.5%
- Purchases 10%
- Payroll 55%

HOW TO DEMONSTRATE THE PROFIT CIRCLE

Using a flip chart, draw a huge circle and then ask your team to split into groups and list the possible expenses you have as a manager/owner. It will surprise them to learn just how many costs there are that they have never even considered.

Then, ask them to guess what your net profit percentage is as a percentage of turnover. Again, they will usually tend to overestimate how much money you are making. You can then reveal the figures.

Do not do this as a 'sob story', merely use it to get them to consider what costs you have and what expenses there are when running or owning a salon – it is a great eye-opener. You can then explain how stock wastage and little elements that may be in their control can lead to the difference between profit and loss. Show how a lack of profitability could affect them; reviewing salaries, refitting, advertising, PR and purchasing new equipment are all things we can do when we are making enough money.

SUMMARY

Reading and understanding a P&L is an essential part of ensuring your business is profitable. It is not just a job for your accountant or book-keeper. Even if you do not have a mathematical brain, try to develop an analytical one so you can understand the key percentages and get a real feel for how the costs are made up.

As with all your managerial duties, they are only truly effective if they are done regularly and accurately – so make sure you get into the habit of compiling and acting on your P&L at the end of every period. The longer you leave it to look at things, the more likelihood there is that they will remain at the back of your mental in-tray and changes will not be instigated in time to make an impact.

CHAPTER 11
STOCK, CAPITAL EXPENDITURE AND SALON DESIGN

In this chapter, we will look at procedures to monitor, track and evaluate your stock spend and effective stocktaking methods. We will consider capital expenditure – large items or expenses that you will have to fund, like shop-fitting and refurbishments – and how these affect your profitability and become assets. We will also cover the salon interior and aspects of salon design and the security systems you will need to have in place to provide a safe environment for your customers and your team.

STOCK CONTROL

Although stock may only account for about 10% of your spending and may not be your biggest cost, it is wise to get have knowledge of some systems to help you control its usage, as it is a significant expense and one that we can impact and control quite easily. There are several ways in which you can track and monitor your stock use, and all will involve regular stocktaking at some level. You can choose to use:

- a stocktaking book
- a computer system for recording stock sales by barcode/scanner
- a mixture of both systems.

Stock-keeping unit (SKU)

A unit of product which is different from another product. For example, a brand sells 'X Brand Long lasting nail polish' which may have 48 different colours therefore there will be 48 SKUs (pronounced skews)

Regardless of which system you use, you will need to track the following (to coincide with your month/period end):

- **stock-keeping unit** (SKU) details – cost price (net), size (such as 100ml) and brand
- stock at commencement of the period
- stock grid – the level or amount of stock you have decided you should hold of the item
- stock ordered (and invoiced for) during the period
- stock received during the period
- stock at the end of the period (carried forward to the next period) – this is your stockholding.

STOCK CONTROL SYSTEMS

Getting your stock control correct is an art. There is a fine balance between being overstocked, and tying up too much capital in your stockholding, and having too little product choice for operators to do their jobs properly or to appeal to potential purchasers. Nobody wants to buy anything from an empty-looking shelf. A good stock control system will monitor the movement of stock throughout the salon, but you will get a feel for what you should be ordering the more you stick to your system and the more regularly and accurately you stocktake. You will also know when usage is too frequent once you become familiar with the ordering and monitoring procedure.

SOFTWARE SYSTEMS

If you are using a software system, you should be able to assess how much retail stock you have sold; it may be coded to be read by a scanner or barcode at the point of sale and therefore tracked automatically. Such software can also trigger automatic reorders, so be sure you set your grid and stock levels correctly and check them regularly.

If you do choose to use stock management software, remember to include the bulk or professional stock; it may be that your system is only capable of tracking retail products and salon-size products need manual stock values calculated. Professional stock will be more difficult to measure as items are probably being replenished from a stock room. This is why a general valuation of the total stock consumed in the period should represent the correct and budgeted proportion of your expenditure, and the right percentage of your turnover and costs. There will be disparities in these general amounts, such as stocking a new range and spending on opening orders, or using significant amounts of stock for marketing and promotional events or offers; but, in general, try and stick to your 10% guideline.

TRACKING TRENDS

If you stocktake accurately and regularly, you will soon see patterns and trends emerging – best-selling lines, slow movers, and so on, should be evident. This will help you set your stock levels, and then ordering can be simplified so you can simply replenish stock which has been used or sold. Remember to track lines which are not moving at all and negotiate uplifts or credits from suppliers before stock becomes too old (use-by dates will be on the product) or tatty to do anything with.

Do not forget to include your semiconsumables. These are items that need replacing every so often, but are not deemed as equipment, such as tint brushes, couch covers, headbands, etc. Personal tools need not be recorded as these invariably belong to the operator, but do note down any ancillary retail you might sell, such as brushes. All these items were a cost to the salon when they were purchased, so they should be recorded in the value of your stockholding (and remember this should match your sums insured, too).

DAILY WORKING STOCK

You need to have a daily working stock in your general working areas, such as your dispensary or colour mixing area, or in each beauty room. Each operator can have their 'working stock' quota and restock it at the beginning or end of their working day from the main stock storage area, such as a stockroom. These areas should be locked –for security reasons, but also because of health and safety – so that only trained operators can access any hazardous substances.

DOCUMENTING STOCK

Most companies have online ordering facilities now but, if not, they will provide order forms. Depending on the size of your custom, a representative (rep) from the company may visit you personally to take your order and inform you of new products and lines. They will then give you a copy of the order placed for your records, this you can cross-reference against the advice note (if applicable, this is sometimes issued to confirm the order). You will normally receive a delivery note when the order arrives, and then the invoice will be sent shortly afterwards. If some items are out of stock they are often marked 'to follow' – this can sometimes result in more paperwork for you so let your rep know if you do not want this to happen (the item will then show as o/s – out of stock).

Late payments on your part will reduce your bargaining power when you are looking for deals from your supplier; don't forget to pay on time!

Invoices

Invoices should list (terms of payment are also usually listed):

- your trading name and address
- account number
- order date
- tax invoice date (this will determine when the amount is entered for accounting purposes, for instance on your VAT return)
- an order number
- the net price per SKU
- a list of the order, per SKU
- details of payment and VAT charged
- any delivery charges.

Invoices should then be entered into the invoice book.

Terms are normally 30 days net, so if you are invoiced on 20 March, you will have to pay the bill on 20 April (one calendar month later). It may be possible to negotiate longer terms, of say 60 days, 90 days or 120 days maximum. Most suppliers in our sector stick to 30 days credit, although new suppliers may issue a **pro-forma invoice**.

DOS AND DON'TS OF STOCK CONTROL

Do:

- delegate some responsibility; a team member can help you count stock while you record the data, for instance
- store hazardous substances in locked areas and follow safety procedures – heavy, bulky items should be at floor level
- review your set stockholding levels regularly and keep on top of potential changes
- Set agreed working stock levels with your operators so replacement of stock is monitored

Pro-forma invoice

This requires payment in advance before goods are delivered. It is normally issued before a trading history has been established or terms have been agreed. You should only normally pay pro-forma if you do not have a track record with a new supplier.

- remember that it is foolish to think that all our teams will always use stock economically, so regularly track wastage if you are getting through too much product
- store stock in rows and by brand so it is easier to reorder and see at a glance what has been used; make sure storage conditions are suitable, for instance temperature levels
- regularly evaluate lines and SKUs – every product in your stockroom or on your retail shelf is costing you money
- sell off any old or slow-moving lines if it is not possible to uplift – tatty, dusty stock makes a retail area very unappealing.

Don't:
- forget to allow staff to buy stock from you at subsidised rates (ie for the price that you pay for them) to avoid possible theft or wastage
- omit your stocktaking; it is a critical gauge of a substantial cost, and regular and accurate information and record keeping will highlight any security problems or overuse
- scrimp on your professional stock – you must not compromise your professionalism or brand values by reusing product if this would not be hygienic.

CAPITAL EXPENDITURE

Capital expenditure

Capital expenditure is incurred when a business spends money either to acquire or upgrade their assets.

We looked in Book 1 at the main ways of financing new equipment, but it will be necessary for your accountant or book-keeper to treat any **capital expenditure** in the correct manner for tax purposes. Capital expenditure is a term used to define spending a business's capital (money) on buying a fixed asset, so it refers to money spent on items rather than the day-to-day running expenses of the business. Capital expenditure is incurred when a business spends money either to buy fixed assets (an asset to the business which is not liquid, like cash) or to add to the value of an existing fixed asset. Equipment, computers, furniture, and such like, are all classed as fixed assets and they are deemed to have a lifespan which extends beyond the taxable year so they have to be accounted for during their whole useful life. Capital expenditure (often referred to as capex) is therefore a term used when a company acquires or upgrades its assets.

Depreciation

An asset which is spread over several years' accounts – or depreciated, to reflect its gradual decline in value .

Assets which have a long but limited lifespan are then capitalised – added to the company's asset account. The full cost of the asset is not deducted in the year in which it is paid for, but is spread over several years' accounts, or **depreciated**, to reflect its gradual decline in value and allow your book-keeper or accountant to 'write off' the expense over a period of time. Assets cannot necessarily be revalued every year, so a nominal figure can be used to show their declining value in the salon's accounts during the course of their salon lifespan.

REINVESTMENT AND REFURBISHMENT

It is essential to keep your salon looking fresh and to stay on top of maintenance, but it will also be necessary to purchase new equipment on a regular basis; for instance, to keep on top of new innovations and services, and to refurbish the salon regularly. Aside from keeping up with the paintwork and general maintenance, an average salon needs complete redecoration at least every 5 years – depending on the footfall and traffic and general levels of wear and tear that come with heavy usage. Every 10 years, it will be necessary to allow for larger items of expenditure such as new sections, beauty couches, manicure stools, chairs, etc, or at least reupholstery or refurbishing of existing equipment.

Much will depend on your brand positioning but, even if you are pitching at the low-end, mass market, you will need to ensure that equipment such as trolleys, mirrors, etc, and salon furniture are all presentable and fit for purpose. Internal décor, such as wallpaper and paintwork, should be clean and fresh and will realistically need replacement every few years, particularly in heavily used areas.

Reinvestment into these core areas should always be ongoing and must be budgeted for in your P&L plan, not least to cover any emergency 'capex' items which may be needed because of damage through fire or flood, or even just to allow for equipment breakdown. Something invariably crops up, so make sure your maintenance budget has a cushion to allow for any emergencies.

THE SALON INTERIOR

The interior of your salon is the biggest reflection of your brand image and the ethos you are trying to create. Productive space should be maximised but not at the expense of the UXP (user experience). Cramming too many rooms or sections into the main working areas may give the client the feeling of a mass production line and lead to impersonal service; yet not using space which could generate income will result in a loss of potential turnover. Getting the right mix is crucial – and will also help to create the ambience and mood of the salon. Close proximity of sections and rooms will result in a 'buzzy' atmosphere, but the client experience may suffer for those looking for peace and tranquillity. Careful planning, along with a real understanding of your customer service experience, is therefore essential.

There are several things to consider when replanning or mapping out your interior and we will look at each of these in turn.

STYLE AND AMBIENCE

Research different retailers like hotels and restaurants for some good ideas and design inspiration. Take elements of a design ethos that appeals and make them visible in your interior design.

Style and ambience are crucial. Nothing says more about your salon than the style of its interior and the more attention to detail you pay to the little things, like fresh flowers or plumped-up cushions, the more you can pitch your brand as a high end alternative. Make sure that whatever 'feel' you try and create is appealing to your target client. For instance, going for a dark and sultry, funky interior is fine if you are trying to establish your brand as youthful and cutting edge; but if your clients are older and more discerning, they will be looking for a salon that reflects their style and taste, and the classic look might be a safer option. There are several interior styles you could choose from:

- contemporary
- boutique
- retro or niche
- boudoir
- cool and trendy, funky
- classic
- modern with a contemporary twist, etc.

Whatever style you decide on, remember that your branding, prices, ethos and whole salon image should reflect the client you are aiming to attract.

COLOUR

The colour of the salon walls and furnishings can create a mood and ambience all of their own. Pick something muted and peaceful for maximum shelf life. Bright or vivid colours can be difficult to patch up and maintain and can look dated quite quickly. Strong colours can also throw off colour hues which may be detrimental to intricate work, such as colouring, and could interfere with technical judgements.

If you are choosing wallpaper, make sure you have several spare rolls for maintenance. Use darker colours for upholstery to show minimum damage and wear and tear, but be prepared to reupholster when necessary to keep the interior fresh looking.

WORK STATIONS

Work stations should be well-placed and situated with enough space between to allow for a staff member to work on a client either side and get to their client all the way around. Make sure you have plenty of electrical sockets (you can never have too many!). Storage is really important in the day-to-day working environment; make sure there is plenty of room to store necessary equipment and that units are lockable, so if staff are stationed in particular areas they can leave their equipment in one place. Giving operators their own working areas helps them to take more responsibility for the appearance of their work station.

TREATMENT ROOMS

Treatment rooms should ideally have natural light or, if not, several lighting options – brighter for close work, and mood lighting, such as dimmer switches, for relaxing treatments. There should be enough room to work all the way around the couch (allowing for trolleys too). If you want to conduct body treatments you will need nearby shower facilities. Think about air conditioning or comfort cooling too. Being too cold or too hot is not conducive to a relaxing treatment. Noise levels are vital also, so sound-proofing walls and doors may be necessary.

LIGHTING

Lighting is critical, especially in a colour department. Look for areas where there is natural lighting, so ideally you should have lots of windows or skylights. Speak to a lighting designer about the different colour tones that can result from using strip or halogen lighting and aim for a lighting scheme that replicates natural light as much as possible. How a client feels when sitting in front of the mirror is crucial – if lighting is too harsh and bright (think about fast food outlets) the client will not feel they look their best, which may not be conducive to spending lots of time enjoying services and treatments.

FLOORS

Experiment and look at as many salon floors as possible until you find an ideal. Dark floors need not necessarily be more practical and wood can stain. Get a sample tile and experiment with different salon substances to be sure of durability – acetone, non-acetone, tint, bleach, artificial red colour pigment, henna, etc, are all a good test and indication of the robustness of a floor. Choose one that can sustain the maximum amount of damage and is easy to clean; remember that tile grouting will be hard to keep fresh looking. Vinyl can create heel marks and imprints and not be as hard-wearing as tiles. In beauty areas, wax spillages can be notoriously difficult to remove, so ensure you choose a durable floor covering that has been tried and tested.

BACKWASHES

For some clients, the backwash experience is as important as the hairdressing service. Look into investing in some lie-down or reclining backwashes to enable you to offer conditioning treatments as a service in their own right. Chair-like backwashes which tilt clients at the neck may be a health and safety risk and there has been speculation that they can cause strokes by trapping nerves (although this unproven), so ensure you look at the latest research and technology and choose a trusted option.

RETAIL

Detail the price point and USP of the product on shelf-descriptors – what the product is, what it does and how much it costs.

The retail area should be easily accessible, well laid out and adequately stocked like any other successful shop or retail outlet. It should be clean, easy to shop and merchandised into rows, which are regularly rearranged to keep the stock looking fresh. Sales invariably take an up-turn if merchandising is changed or moved around, so make it a calendar duty to rearrange your stock regularly. Retailing units should be bright and well lit, with eye-level shelving well-utilised with best-selling products for maximum appeal and to make the most of potential turnover. Shelf talkers work well for highlighting specific products; again, selecting by rotation works best, and ideally tying in with your marketing and promotions calendar.

STAFF AREAS

A good staff area is vital and should contain a table and chairs for eating, bench seating, natural lighting if possible and good ventilation. Providing storage such as lockers will help to keep the salon clutter free, and it is worth thinking about putting in a fridge, microwave and sink (if you do not have separate catering facilities) to enable staff to bring in food from home if there's no time to go out for lunch.

DISPENSARY/STOCKROOM

Open-plan mixing areas can work well in colour departments and create a focal point. Nail colour merchandising units work well in spas to create a point of interest but also act as a general stockholding facility, too. Behind the scenes, make sure that there is sufficient light, ventilation and washing (as well as hand-washing) facilities for the correct professional usage of products, and keep a working stock only in such areas. Stockrooms should be lockable and spacious, with plenty of movable shelving for flexibility and rearrangement. Stock should be stored by rotation, with newest orders automatically moved to the back of the row so that older stock is being used up first.

THE CLIENT JOURNEY FLOW

Ideally, the salon interior should follow the flow of the client journey through the salon, so that all client-facing areas are easily accessible and feel spacious and uncramped. Think about your customer's journey – it starts at reception for checking in and waiting, then to the cloakroom area, ideally with nearby toilets and other facilities such as a refreshment area, then follows a natural progression either straight to the treatment area or via the backwash or colour zone for hairdressing. After the service, it is back to the reception via the retail area to encourage home care and finally finishing with bill paying and, hopefully, rebooking.

Think about how well your salon space is cohesive with this flow and, when thinking about design, make sure it fits as well as possible. For example, retail should not be located too far away from reception and the waiting area should be located where reception staff can spot any forgotten clients. Staff and storage areas should be located in space which otherwise could not be properly utilised productively. You should make sure they are at the back or in badly configured areas so you are making the most of your best floor space. Your expertise will be more important than an independent architect who may not understand the client experience at the same level as those who are in the profession, so make sure you have input into any professional feedback you may get on the layout.

Clients respond favourably to spaces being clear and identifiable. If, for instance, you are creating a manicure/pedicure area, make sure it does not appear to be an 'afterthought'. You should set up a proper area so the space is zoned or themed and the customer instantly recognises where she is and why she is there. It will give your treatments more credibility and allow for a significantly greater client following if you invest in the correct equipment. Avoid 'playing at it'; this will not encourage an uptake in the treatment or service you want to establish, whereas looking serious about what you are doing, and having the right area to back it up, will.

SECURITY PROCEDURES

As the salon manager or owner, you have a duty of care to provide safe, secure surroundings for both your customers to enjoy and your team to work in. Many salons have CCTV (closed circuit TV) recording and monitoring equipment, both to prevent staff from pilfering and to ensure customer theft is kept to a minimum. CCTV also acts as a powerful deterrent for any robberies or other criminal activity that could occur, particularly in small salons where a full-time receptionist may not always be in evidence.

Make sure you have assigned key-holders who may be named on your insurance policy. It is worth investing in an alarm to ensure optimum safety. In some central or urban locations, it may be prudent to think about installing a panic button behind reception and display signs indicating CCTV is in operation.

You also need to think about the client's security during their visit. Make sure they are aware that you do not take responsibility for personal belongings, for instance in the cloakroom, or during treatments when they remove valuable items such as jewellery. Ensure that all staff are aware of your policies, and display clear signs so the client knows the ownership of safeguarding their belongings lies with them.

SUMMARY

Stockholding needs regular evaluation – find the methods that work for you and ensure you track your stock usage accurately and devise a system of both looking after and repurchasing your goods.

Reinvestment in your interior is critical to your brand positioning. Budget accordingly, so you can allow for regular refurbishments and can afford to maintain your salon correctly and with attention to detail. Consult your team to ensure you have taken care of the practicalities – not just the aesthetics – when revamping your salon or rearranging your working areas, taking the client journey into account.

Capital expenditure will be your greatest significant investment so plan for ways of financing large items of equipment. You should discuss how you will monetise these items in your accounts/financial statements with your book-keeper or accountant.

CHAPTER 12
UNDERSTANDING YOUR FINANCIAL STATEMENTS, STATUTORY AND AUDITED ACCOUNTS

This final chapter will look at a set of sample financial statements, their formats and structures, and the terms used, to give you a real understanding of your financial practice. We will explain some of the language used by your accountant and some of the calculations made in order to compile your-end-of year financial accounts. This will give you a clear understanding of how they have assessed your financial performance.

FINANCIAL STATEMENTS

TYPES OF FINANCIAL STATEMENT

You might be a sole trader, in partnership or have a limited company but you will need to compile a set of financial statements at the end of each trading year. The financial statements will have a standard format and, in the case of limited companies, will be determined by the law and therefore statutory.

There are three types of financial statement: statutory accounts, audited accounts and financial statements.

Statutory accounts

These are the fixed format for publishing financial statements. The make-up and appearance of statutory accounts is legally determined.

Audited accounts

These are statutory accounts that have been independently checked and verified by a firm of auditors. They are mandatory after the business reaches a certain level, or voluntary until that level is reached.

Financial statements

These are for sole traders or partnerships; they are a formatted version of your end-of-year trading statements that will form part of your personal tax computations and liabilities.

Unless you are a limited company, and are therefore required to file accounts at Companies House for the public record, you are not necessarily obligated to produce financial statements for your business. But there is an implied element of conviction and professionalism if you do submit these documents with your tax computations, as they will form part of the calculation of your tax liabilities if you are a sole trader or a partnership. They will also give you a clearer idea of your true financial situation.

USEFUL TERMS FOUND IN YOUR STATEMENT

We will now look at some of the terms used to help you better understand your statements.

Assets and liabilities

Assets are defined as one of two things:
- something you own – buildings, goods, brand names, shares, money, land and so on, or
- something you are owed by someone else – such as money.

A **liability** is something you owe to someone else and expect to hand over in due course, ie money.

Your **net assets** are what you would have left if you sold off all your assets and paid off all your liabilities; your net assets are what you are worth or the value 'due' to the shareholders.

There are some other terms that you need to become familiar with:
- **fixed assets** are any assets which the company uses on a long-term basis (as opposed to assets that are bought by the company and sold on to customers), such as buildings, equipment, etc
- **current assets** are assets you expect to sell or turn into cash within one year, eg stock
- **current liabilities** are liabilities that you expect to pay within the next year, eg amounts owed to suppliers
- **long-term liabilities** are liabilities that you expect to have to pay, but not within the next year.

Accruals and profit

Accruals are any costs that you have not been billed for yet, but know you will have to pay and which have to be recognised. Adjustments are made at the end of an accounting period to recognise expenses that have been incurred during the period but for which no invoice has yet been issued.

Gross profit is the difference between the total value of sales and the cost of providing the sales.

Operating profit is the gross profit after the operating expenses have also been deducted.

Profit before tax is the profit left after paying any interest to the lenders, but before corporation tax (net profit).

Profit after tax is the profit remaining after taxes, such as corporation tax.

Someone, either a third party or the shareholders, has a claim over each and every asset of the company. Therefore, whatever happens, the assets must always equal the claims over the assets: this is the fundamental principal of accounting.

(Source: Accounts Demystified by Anthony Rice)

Balance sheet

A **balance sheet** is a statement listing all a company's assets and liabilities and their value at a particular point in time (at the end of their financial year). Think of it as a 'freeze frame' of your salon business at a particular time; it shows a company's financial position at any given moment. Various adjustments are required before the balance sheet accurately reflects the company's financial position. All entries are made using 'double entry' so that the balance sheet always balances.

The balance sheet will ultimately show two things:
1   the net assets of the business
2   an explanation of what the net assets represent to the shareholders – there are two main elements to this:
   a)   the money the shareholders invested in the company
   b)   the company made a profit, a certain amount of which was retained (rather than paid out to the shareholders).

THE FORMAT OF STATEMENTS

Most accounting statements use the same accounting principles and there will be little difference in format between the types of end-of-year statements you compile. Each page will state the company or business name, with the trading year being referred to at the top of the page.

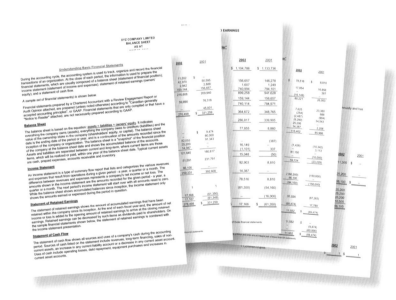

There are several sections:
- officers and professional advisors
- Director's report
- profit and loss account
- balance sheet
- notes to the financial statements.

The following sections will also appear, but do not form part of the financial statements:
- detailed profit and loss account
- notes to the detailed profit and loss account.

OFFICERS AND PROFESSIONAL ADVISORS

In this section, the following people will be listed, together with their addresses:
- board of directors
- company secretary
- registered office
- accountants
- bankers.

DIRECTOR'S REPORT

Here, the statements will list the principal activities of the company or business, the directors who served during the financial year, confirmation of the registered office, name and signature of the company secretary and the date of approval of the statements and signature.

PROFIT AND LOSS ACCOUNT

On this page, the following items are shown in two columns as a year-end total, listing the current financial year and the same information from the previous year's financial statements for comparison. Notes to which the sums refer are listed in the 'Notes' column.
- **turnover**
  - cost of sales (payroll and stock)
- **gross profit** (turnover less cost of sales)
  - administrative expenses
  - other operating income
- **operating profit**
  - interest receivable
- **profit on ordinary activities before taxation**
  - tax on profit on ordinary activities
- **profit for the financial year.**

BALANCE SHEET ITEMS

Here, the following items are shown, again in two comparable columns showing the previous statement's performance against the current financial year. Again, the notes to which the sums refer are listed in a separate column.

Fixed assets

Fixed assets can be tangible (physical – something you can see or touch) or intangible (like the value of goodwill or a brand). Intangible assets cannot be physically touched. Fixed assets include equipment, machinery and so on that give value to the business over a period; these are tangible assets.

Current assets

A current asset is an asset that is expected to be turned into cash within one year of the balance sheet date. Current assets could be:

- stocks (value of the stockholding at the end of the financial year)
- debtors (people who owe the business money in whatever form – salons don't tend to have a great deal of debtors as most customers pay at the time of service, but this could include credit notes or retrospective discount from suppliers or invoices that are raised but not paid at the end of the financial year)
- cash at bank and in hand (for example, reconciled bank balance and the cash balance of a petty cash tin, if applicable – the total amount of money in the bank – it does not have to be physical cash; cash is just the term used for ready money).

Creditors

Creditors are people to whom you may owe money, for example trade creditors such as suppliers, or other creditors such as bank loans, overdrafts, VAT, PAYE, corporation tax or NICs, etc. These are not necessarily payments that you have missed but amounts that may be outstanding at your end-of-year cut-off date. This will include amounts falling due within one year.

Net current assets

This is the total of your current assets, less your creditors.

Total assets less current liabilities

This sum is your total overall assets, including your fixed assets. It can indicate the financial long-term health of the company.

Provision for liabilities

These are liabilities that are going to be falling due after more than one year. For example, if you own the lease and you have to make a provision for dilapidations in five years' time, you can make a provision now.

Capital and reserves

This section includes the following:

- called-up equity share capital – only applicable to limited companies, this figure relates to the nominal value of the shares issued to the shareholders
- other reserves – sometimes shares are issued at a premium (not a nominal value, such as £1) and this is shown separately as a share premium reserve
- profit and loss account – the accumulated profits of the business that have not been paid out by way of dividend to the shareholders.

Shareholders' funds

This is the total of the share capital and reserves –only applicable to limited companies.

After the balance sheet, the directors' statement is included and directors must sign to acknowledge their responsibilities and compliance to the Companies Act 2006. The company registration number is listed here, if applicable.

FURTHER ANALYSIS

From the information in your balance sheet, there can be a breakdown of the items in greater detail for further analysis.

NOTES TO THE FINANCIAL STATEMENTS

The notes to the accounts help to make sense of the balance sheet and how it has been calculated. Again, split into two columns for the current and previous year's financial statements, the information here will include peculiarities pertaining to the following accounting policies.

ACCOUNTING POLICIES

Basis of accounting

The basis of accounting explains when accounts were compiled to (date) and the methods of how you have accounted for the items listed (as there may be more than one possible treatment of the expenditure).

Turnover

The turnover and how it was derived, ie net of VAT.

Fixed assets

This notes the fixed assets that were initially recorded at cost.

Depreciation

This is an explanation of the depreciation calculation (how the depreciation has been worked out). It involves writing off the cost of a tangible fixed asset, less its estimated residual value, over the useful economic life of the asset. For instance, leasehold properties and how the value of the lease has been depreciated will be listed here. Fixtures, fittings and equipment, for example, may be depreciated over four, five or 10 years, and motor vehicles at 25% per annum.

Stocks

This is your stockholding and how it has been valued and calculated.

Operating lease agreements

This covers any lease-purchase, hire-purchase and so on, and provides explanations of how such financed items have been accounted for.

Deferred taxation

Items are treated differently for taxation purposes from how they are for accounting purposes, which can give rise to possible future potential tax liabilities. The policy here explains how your accountant or book-keeper has accounted for, or treated, such items.

Financial instruments

This refers to more complex ways of financing your business, ie some form of structured bank loan or other debt, if applicable.

Other operating income

This is income received that is incidental to your main business, such as rent received from subletting.

Operating profit

This is profit before interest and corporation tax, so helps to compare a business which has had bank investment (paying interest charges) with a business which has shareholders' investment.

Directors' remuneration

This includes whatever salaries and benefits are being paid to directors. Even if they are showing in your payroll costs, you must make a separate disclosure of any remuneration.

Interest receivable

This is bank interest, or other interest, on any deposits which may be held.

Taxation on ordinary activities
This is taxation on profit made after interest has been deducted, ie corporation tax and the rate at which it was paid.

Dividends
For limited companies only, these are the profits paid out to the shareholders. How much was paid will be listed here.

Tangible fixed assets
From your balance sheet, this is a further analysis of what is in your fixed assets, split into separate headings such as leasehold properties, fixtures, fittings and equipment and motor vehicles, and a total column:

- **cost** – for the year, by separate areas, ie what was spent
- **depreciation** – both to date and for the financial year, again in separate areas/columns
- **net book value** – this is the original cost, less what has already been written off.

Debtors and creditors
Debtors are people who owe the company money.

Creditors are people to whom the company owes money.

Deferred taxation
This is the balance between the excess of taxation allowances and the depreciation on fixed assets.

OTHER PROVISIONS

These include the following terms.

Commitment under operating leases
This applies to leaseholders and relates to disclosure of the length of time remaining and the cost of the remaining commitment.

Related party transactions
This is a statutory obligation to disclose transactions with parties connected with the company and the inclusion of any balances owed to or from that party (such as a separate company which may have links with or has been funded by the parent company).

Authorised share capital
This is the maximum number of shares issuable and gives a breakdown of the issued shares (allotted shares) by director/individual.

Reserves

These are values that are not part of your trading account, like revaluation reserves. For example, if you own a building and the value has increased, you need to show this profit on your balance sheet.

DETAILED PROFIT AND LOSS ACCOUNT

In this section, there will be more information about the salon's performance. Here the figures will match, in theory, your management accounting P&Ls. However, for greater accuracy, they will be calculated in a similar way to your financial statements and so will include figures that you will not normally work out, like your gross profit and your operating profit. Do not, therefore, be alarmed if there are slight differences.

Items will again be listed in two columns, comparing the current financial year with the previous one. Firstly, there will be a one-page statement detailing the total income and expenditure. Each column will show income on the left and expenditure on the right so you can easily see which is an 'in' and which is an 'out'.

TERMS USED

Turnover
This is turnover net of VAT.

Cost of sales
This includes the following:
- opening stock and work in progress (this is just your last year's closing stock carried forward, as in our industry there is no work in progress normally; it generally refers to manufacturing, when goods are partially made)
- purchases and consumables (stock)
- wages and salaries (total payroll costs including HMRC/NICs)
- closing stock (stock holding).

Gross profit
This is your turnover, less cost of sales.

Overheads
This includes all administrative expenses (all other running costs).

Other operating income
This is rent receivable.

Operating profit
This is bank interest receivable (across all bank accounts).

Profit on ordinary activities

This is the amount of net profit.

Then, in a similar format to our management P&L, the expenditure and income will be listed in more detail. However, it will usually be itemised slightly differently, and broken down into the following categories.

ADMINISTRATIVE EXPENSES

These will include the following types of costs and expenses.

Personnel costs

Personnel costs will be your payroll and any other perks for staff (broken down separately):

- directors' remuneration
- health insurance
- directors' pensions
- administrative staff salaries.

Establishment expenses

These are costs that relate to the premises:

- rent, rates and water
- light and heat
- insurance
- repairs and maintenance.

General expenses

These are other 'outs' taken from your P&L:

- motor and travel
- telephone
- staff training and courses
- computer costs
- office expenses
- postage and stationery
- sundry expenses
- laundry and cleaning
- advertising and promotion
- entertaining
- legal and professional
- accountancy fees
- depreciation and amortisation (assets and items of capital expenditure that your accountant has depreciated or amortised appear here as an expense).

Financial costs

These include:

- bank charges
- credit card commission.

Think of your profit in various levels –gross profit, operating profit, profit before tax (net profit), and profit after tax. It does not really matter that you only really understand net profit through compiling your management accounts, as long as you are monitoring and getting to grips with the one that really matters!

Interest receivable

This is bank interest receivable (across all bank accounts).

(Source: *Paul Mattei, LLP*)

CASH FLOW

Cash flow is the change in a company's balance over a particular period; and its **operating cash flow** is the cash flow that is solely due to enterprise (disregarding interest, etc). I always think of a business's cash flow as its liquidity (although this technically means the ability of a company to pay its short-term liabilities) but it conjures up a helpful image of the money that is flowing through the bank account. When we refer to 'cash' flow we are not talking necessarily about cash or sterling – it could be any bank income, like credit cards, for instance. Basically, it is money that you have not had to wait for – as fewer people pay with cash and more and more customers pay by card, you do not need to think of it in terms of actual cash.

USEFUL ACCOUNTING TERMS

Some other accounting terms you may hear, or may need to understand when communicating with your bank or accountant, include the following.

Audit trail – is the trail of tracking transactions in chronological order across the company's accounting system. For instance, rather than deleting a void transaction, a proper audit trail will record it then show the reverse transaction so the ledgers balance.

Amortisation – sometimes intangible assets are amortised (whereas tangible assets are depreciated). This is the amount by which the book value (the value of the asset the company has on its books) is deemed to have fallen during a particular accounting period, ie the asset is systematically written down in value over an agreed period of time.

Book value – the value an asset has in a company's books.

Gearing (also known as leverage) – this is the ratio of debt to equity that funds a company.

Market value – this is the value of an asset to an unconnected third party.

Net worth – the total assets of the company, less its liabilities.

Nominal ledger – each of the balance sheet items makes up the nominal account, and all the nominal accounts make up the nominal ledger.

Posting – entering a transaction into the relevant ledgers; it is the date when it is entered into the company's balance sheet.

Provision – an expense recognised in the accounts for a particular accounting period to allow for expected losses.

Purchase ledger – lists and records all invoices, like an invoice book would, either manually or by computer.

Price earnings ratio – this is the share price divided by earnings per share (historic, current or future – potentially). This sum is used as the formula for which multiples are calculated when valuing companies.

Ordinary share – this is the most common class of share, which entitles the holder to a proportional share of dividends and net assets, and to vote at meetings of the shareholders.

Trial balance is a listing of the nominal accounts, showing a balance for each.

Write up/down/off – revaluing an asset (upwards, downwards or down to zero).

(Source: *Accounts Demystified* by Anthony Rice)

SUMMARY

It is essential to have an understanding of the terms you will see in your financial statements if you want to know how your book-keeper or accountant has treated your expenditure for tax purposes. You do not need to be a trainee accountant to get familiar with the terms (although it might help!) but make sure you take time to read through your financial statements at the end of each year. Do not be afraid to ask questions so that you understand the basics. You do not have to remember all the details – just refer back to this guide as and when you need to.

Financial statements are no substitute for the management accounts you will need to do as you go along to keep track of your spending and profitability. Waiting until your accountant or book-keeper presents you with your statements sometime after your year end will not enable you to make any impact on your profitability – so ensure your P&L and analysis sheets are what you use to guide you through your finances. In doing so, your financial statements will merely become an interesting look at how your taxation has been treated and not an action plan for the future.

STEPS FOR SUCCESS

10 STEPS TO A PROFITABLE SALON

1 Know your target market – market, brand and promote yourself to suit your client. Survey regularly. Act on feedback.

2 Monitor the competition. Experience their services. Mystery shop.

3 Analyse and track business performance in all areas. Manage and act on what you monitor.

4 Identify, strengthen and focus on core services and areas of turnover. Market and promote weaker areas.

5 Monitor and track team performance and reward/incentivise them accordingly.

6 Communicate financial information with your team and involve them in the business decision-making.

7 Streamline your team so fewer staff are more productive and earn larger salaries.

8 Have realistic profit expectations and set yourself achievable long-term goals in bite-sized pieces.

9 Create budgets and net targets around fixed costs and overheads and frequently negotiate and re-evaluate variable costs.

10 Make sure your team share your brand vision and your customer always experiences it.

EPILOGUE

Well done! You have now fully covered all the financial terms and jargon your accountant will bombard you with, or which HMRC may refer to, and you can use this book as a reference guide when you need to.

Understanding the finances does not have to be difficult; it comes down to getting to grips with what is coming in and what is going out. Even the world's greatest business gurus and entrepreneurs will tell us that making profit boils down to the difference between the two – so do not get too anxious about the technical terms.

Hopefully, using some of the tips and hints in my book will help you to gain a real understanding of making money in your salon. Whether you are the owner and we are discussing your money, or you are the manager and your salary is dependent on the financial performance of your salon, you will want it to be profitable.

It is not enough to feign a lack of understanding about your salon's finances – if you know how the money works you can have an impact on making more of it; knowledge is always power.

In the first book of this series, Getting Established, we covered all the legalities and red tape that you have to consider when opening or starting up your salon; and it will act as a handy reference guide when you want to check back to make sure you have covered everything.

In the third book of the Ultimate Salon Management series, Team Performance, we will concentrate on the essential ingredient of any good salon – our operators – and how we can make sure we sustain their performance and, in turn, retain our customers. We will cover interviewing and recruitment, employment obligations and training and developing your team. We will look at customer service and how to track and deliver it, as well as your personal leadership skills and how to develop them. We will also cover disciplinary procedures for when things go awry.

We'll also look at look at monitoring individual performance and what you should track to ensure optimum results from each of your stylists, technicians and therapists – and appraisals, so you can evaluate them. I will give you ideas for salary packages, competitions and incentives, and we will consider career pathing and staff retention, and how to hold on to great team members. Finally, we will look at the effective booking systems you can instigate to maximise our most precious commodity – time. We will finish with my essential 10 steps to success.

By the end of the series, you will know everything necessary to be the most effective salon manager and produce great results for you, your salon, your team and, most importantly, your clients.

INDEX